THE PURPOSEFUL MD

LAURA SUTTIN

THE PURPOSEFUL MD

Creating the Life
You Love
Without Guilt

WBP
WRITING BRAVE PRESS

Writing Brave Press
1940 Palmer Avenue, #1032
Larchmont NY 10538
www.writingbravepress.com

Distributed by IngramSpark

Copyright ©2024 by Laura Suttin, MD

All the necessary due diligence has been made to contact the copyright holders. Anyone who believes that their copyright to be infringed upon is welcome to contact the publisher.

All rights reserved. No part of this book may be reproduced in any form or by any electronic or mechanical means, including information storage and retrieval systems, without written permission from the author, except by a reviewer who may quote passages for review.

Cover and Text Design: Danny Meono
Copyeditor: Meghan Muldowney
Author Photos: Casey McCarty

Library of Congress Cataloging-in-Publication Data available.
ISBN 979-8-9873704-5-2 (Paperback)
ISBN 979-8-9873704-6-9 (eBook)

First Edition

The information provided in this book is intended for physicians and other medical professionals looking to improve their time management skills and overall well-being. While the author is a physician, this book is not a substitute for professional medical advice, diagnosis, or treatment. By reading my book or listening to my podcast, you are not creating a physician/patient relationship with Dr. Suttin. The strategies and techniques mentioned in this book may not be suitable for every individual. It is important to consult with your medical provider before making any significant changes to your lifestyle or routine.

Furthermore, the author does not endorse any specific products or services mentioned in this book and receives no compensation for their promotion. Any examples shared in this book are for illustrative purposes only and should not be taken as medical advice. Names mentioned are also for illustration purposes only, and names may be changed from any real patient to protect their privacy.

LAURA SUTTIN

THE PURPOSEFUL MD

Creating the Life
You Love
Without Guilt

WBP
WRITING BRAVE PRESS

Writing Brave Press
1940 Palmer Avenue, #1032
Larchmont NY 10538
www.writingbravepress.com

Distributed by IngramSpark

Copyright ©2024 by Laura Suttin, MD

All the necessary due diligence has been made to contact the copyright holders. Anyone who believes that their copyright to be infringed upon is welcome to contact the publisher.

All rights reserved. No part of this book may be reproduced in any form or by any electronic or mechanical means, including information storage and retrieval systems, without written permission from the author, except by a reviewer who may quote passages for review.

Cover and Text Design: Danny Meono
Copyeditor: Meghan Muldowney
Author Photos: Casey McCarty

Library of Congress Cataloging-in-Publication Data available.
ISBN 979-8-9873704-5-2 (Paperback)
ISBN 979-8-9873704-6-9 (eBook)

First Edition

The information provided in this book is intended for physicians and other medical professionals looking to improve their time management skills and overall well-being. While the author is a physician, this book is not a substitute for professional medical advice, diagnosis, or treatment. By reading my book or listening to my podcast, you are not creating a physician/patient relationship with Dr. Suttin. The strategies and techniques mentioned in this book may not be suitable for every individual. It is important to consult with your medical provider before making any significant changes to your lifestyle or routine.

Furthermore, the author does not endorse any specific products or services mentioned in this book and receives no compensation for their promotion. Any examples shared in this book are for illustrative purposes only and should not be taken as medical advice. Names mentioned are also for illustration purposes only, and names may be changed from any real patient to protect their privacy.

Dedicated to my father, who, though he is no longer physically present to cheer me on, continues to guide me and support me every day.

Dad, your belief in me has become a part of me, fueling me to never give up on my dreams. Your love and encouragement will forever live on in my heart.

Contents

Introduction..1

My Story..11

Chapter 1: Define Your Why...19

Chapter 2: Clarify Your Goals..31

Chapter 3: Outsmart Your Sneaky Brain......................43

Chapter 4: Take a Small Step...55

Chapter 5: Set and Maintain Boundaries......................65

Chapter 6: Manage Strong Emotions.............................79

Chapter 7: Create Your Own Confidence......................93

Chapter 8: Get the Rest You Need................................101

Chapter 9: Develop More Foundational Habits........109

Chapter 10: Let Go of What's Not Working...............119

Chapter 11: Celebrate Yourself...................................... 129

Chapter 12: You as The Flourishing Physician..........137

Introduction

Amanda is a family physician who completed her residency 3 years ago. She's employed in a busy urban primary care center, caring for a wide variety of patients of all ages. If you had asked her 10 years ago what her "dream job" was, this would have been it. She loves the relationships she creates with her patients, and she cheers for them when they hit their goals and improve their health.

She married her medical school sweetheart, Tim, right after graduation. Tim is a surgical transplant fellow in a nearby hospital. They recently welcomed their first daughter, Chloe, who is 6 months old. Amanda's parents live about 30 minutes away and help occasionally with Chloe, who is in full-time day care.

About a year ago, Amanda and Tim upsized their house in anticipation of expanding their family. Even though they knew it would be a lot of work and expense, they chose a beautiful Craftsman home and moved in a few months before

Chloe was born. Their weekends have been filled with home-related projects, much more than they originally anticipated.

Amanda describes her life as "full" and "blessed." Many days, she also describes it as "overwhelming" and "too busy." She wishes she could spend more time with her husband and daughter. She feels pulled in so many different directions and never feels that there is enough time to do what she *needs* to do, let alone what she *wants* to do. When she was in medical school, she picked up kickboxing and fell in love with the sport, both as exercise and as an outlet for her stress. She longs to attend a kickboxing class nearby, and occasionally looks at the schedule, but feels pangs of guilt when she considers signing up for a class. She spends her days counseling patients on prioritizing healthy habits like sleep and exercise, feeling like a fraud because she knows she's not getting enough of either.

She loves working with patients but finds it difficult to balance her work and home life. Most of Amanda's colleagues are several years older than her, with older children and more established careers, and don't seem to struggle to find balance the way she does. Most of the male physicians have wives who stay home with the children and take care of the home. Amanda feels so much guilt when her day care calls to pick up Chloe because she's running a fever; now she has to ask her partners to cover for her, and disappoint the patients who've waited months to see her. Meanwhile, she wonders why Tim never gets the day care call and never feels that he must drop

Introduction

Amanda is a family physician who completed her residency 3 years ago. She's employed in a busy urban primary care center, caring for a wide variety of patients of all ages. If you had asked her 10 years ago what her "dream job" was, this would have been it. She loves the relationships she creates with her patients, and she cheers for them when they hit their goals and improve their health.

She married her medical school sweetheart, Tim, right after graduation. Tim is a surgical transplant fellow in a nearby hospital. They recently welcomed their first daughter, Chloe, who is 6 months old. Amanda's parents live about 30 minutes away and help occasionally with Chloe, who is in full-time day care.

About a year ago, Amanda and Tim upsized their house in anticipation of expanding their family. Even though they knew it would be a lot of work and expense, they chose a beautiful Craftsman home and moved in a few months before

Chloe was born. Their weekends have been filled with home-related projects, much more than they originally anticipated.

Amanda describes her life as "full" and "blessed." Many days, she also describes it as "overwhelming" and "too busy." She wishes she could spend more time with her husband and daughter. She feels pulled in so many different directions and never feels that there is enough time to do what she *needs* to do, let alone what she *wants* to do. When she was in medical school, she picked up kickboxing and fell in love with the sport, both as exercise and as an outlet for her stress. She longs to attend a kickboxing class nearby, and occasionally looks at the schedule, but feels pangs of guilt when she considers signing up for a class. She spends her days counseling patients on prioritizing healthy habits like sleep and exercise, feeling like a fraud because she knows she's not getting enough of either.

She loves working with patients but finds it difficult to balance her work and home life. Most of Amanda's colleagues are several years older than her, with older children and more established careers, and don't seem to struggle to find balance the way she does. Most of the male physicians have wives who stay home with the children and take care of the home. Amanda feels so much guilt when her day care calls to pick up Chloe because she's running a fever; now she has to ask her partners to cover for her, and disappoint the patients who've waited months to see her. Meanwhile, she wonders why Tim never gets the day care call and never feels that he must drop everything to take care of a sick child.

And the charting…it never ends. She hasn't had a "lunch break" in years. She is never done with charting by the time she has to leave to pick up Chloe. She's frequently rushing through her last patient visit to get to the day care before it closes, and then she feels awful, like she's short-changed that patient.

By the time she picks up Chloe, gets home, starts dinner, and puts Chloe to bed, Amanda is exhausted. All she can think about are the messages in her electronic inbox, and how her patients are waiting for her to respond to refill requests, messages, and referrals. She sacrifices her evenings and any possibility of free time to complete as much charting as she can after Chloe goes to bed. She often falls asleep charting on the couch in the evenings, and when she wakes up, her husband is already asleep. She loves her husband dearly and misses the time they used to spend together as a couple.

Amanda is so confused. She has everything she has ever wanted–to be a primary care physician, a wife, and a mom. She knows she is lucky to have what she has and tells herself she should be grateful. She's "living the dream" as many of her friends and family tell her. This is what she has worked for her whole life!

And yet…she struggles to find joy in the everyday. She is rushing from place to place all the time and never has a moment to herself. She's exhausted, sleep-deprived, and sees no end in sight. She hasn't had a physical in years. She doesn't feel she is clinically depressed but she knows she isn't happy. The feeling that she "should" be happy–and the front she feels she must put on for everyone–makes everything so much more difficult to deal with. She doesn't have many friends close by, and none who are physician moms who would even understand. Her colleagues are at different stages in life and can't relate to her.

∼

If this resonates with you, my dear reader, I am so glad you are reading this. I'll say first and foremost, you are not alone. I'm honored to be sharing this sacred space with you. I share this space with you, with my clients and other physician "sisters," and many other women who feel the same way. Reading this book will take you on a journey through my own story and the stories of some of my coaching clients. You'll come away with the full understanding that there is a better way to live your life–a way to honor what you need and to allow you to create the life you've always wanted.

So many of my physician coaching clients come to me asking for help with time management. As I've come to learn by working with them, and working on my own time management skills, **time management in and of itself is just the tip of the iceberg.** If it were easy, everyone would already be crushing it! What's underneath the surface of the ocean surrounding that iceberg are the other topics we will explore: managing strong emotions, setting boundaries, and creating foundational habits. If you're not sure how those relate to time management, you're not alone–we'll get into it together!

You would not have picked up this book if you hadn't already tried "everything under the sun" to manage your time more effectively. You've probably tried all the techniques and STILL feel like you don't have enough time in the day to accomplish everything you want to accomplish. Yet, when you look back on your life, you KNOW that you've accomplished WAY more than the average person. You likely earned excellent grades in high school, received an undergraduate degree that was strenuous enough to prepare you for medical school, earned a coveted medical school spot, worked your tail off in medical school to match into internship or residency, worked your tail off AGAIN in residency (and possibly a fellowship), completed your training and FINALLY "made it" to the other side–private practice, attending, etc. Oh and along the way, many of you started a family–gaining a partner or spouse, kids, a home, pets, to name a few. You're probably also balancing the needs of aging parents and maintaining adult friendships (which is not as easy as when you were a kid!).

You did it! You're here. It's great, right? *RIGHT?*

Except…maybe it's not as great as they made it out to be. This was supposed to be it! That's what we worked all our lives for! That's what we gave up our twenties for! That's what we put off earning a living wage for!

Somehow, they forgot to tell us how HARD it would be.

There are more responsibilities and more pressure than we ever imagined. There is also room for more immense joy and love and fun than we ever imagined.

Raise your hand if you are telling yourself, "Who has time for joy? Who has time for fun? I've got a full-time job, on-call duties, a spouse, a dog, a mortgage, 3 kids who have to be driven to school and sports and dances, and aging parents who live nearby who are becoming less and less independent. I have NO TIME in the day for ME. I've tried EVERYTHING to squeeze in 'me time.' Bubble baths aren't getting the job done."

If that sounds like you, I wrote this book for you.

You are no stranger to managing your time effectively. You've been doing it all your life. You wouldn't be here if you weren't disciplined with your time. The challenge is the barometer by which you are measuring yourself. You're measuring yourself against an impossible cultural standard that is telling you that you "should" be doing more, sleeping more, exercising more, working more, spending time with your kids more.

What pushed me to write this book was the strong desire to share my story with others who are struggling with the same things. I want you to know two things: first, you are not alone, and second, you can save yourself from further suffering by utilizing the practices discussed in the book.

This book is about much more than time management. You will come away with very concrete steps you can take right now to have more time for whatever your heart desires. You will also learn how to throw away the barometer. You will learn how to quiet the voice telling you what you "should" be doing, so that this voice doesn't drive your behaviors and lead to guilt. By taking the actions described in this book, you'll come away with a new outlook on your environment and on yourself that will be better than you could have ever imagined.

Each chapter includes a "get into action" step at the end, where you will journal on your reflections from the concepts in the chapter, as well as making commitments to yourself. You can find these journaling prompts as a downloadable document at www.thepurposefulmd.com/book. My goal is for you to not just increase your knowledge of the concepts, but to put them into action and truly change your life. **Insight without action does not lead to change; action is what moves us forward, closer to our goals.**

A Few Tips on Journaling

If you are new to journaling, it can be a little intimidating. Many of us harbor some amount of fear of how our writing looks and sounds. We are used to our writing being critiqued and edited. I encourage you to notice that fear, and practice writing as if no one will see this but you…because this is true. Spelling and grammar don't count in a journal. Trying to cultivate a perfect journal entry will hamper your creativity and authenticity (we will work with perfectionism and how to manage through those difficult emotions throughout the book).

(NOTE: Gender terms used in this book. Throughout this text, I use the terms "women" and "men" based on gender roles, rather than based on biological sex assigned at birth. You also may notice that many of the examples cited are based on heteronormative relationships and assumptions. This is because most of the research has been done on cisgender, heterosexual couples and relationships.)

My goal with this book for you is to become a Flourishing Physician. What is a Flourishing Physician?

A Flourishing Physician:
- Knows her worth
- Lives life on her terms
- Lives a life she loves
- Prioritizes herself and her own needs
- Gets enough sleep and wakes up refreshed
- Manages her time and energy in a way that feels authentic
- Doesn't feel guilty spending time on things she enjoys
- Is fully present, no matter what she is doing
- Pursues hobbies and activities that light her up
- Lights her flame so she can light others' flames
- Believes in herself
- Has confidence in herself
- Values herself

Before we get started, I want you to take this moment right now to decide to choose yourself. Decide that you are on a journey to becoming a Flourishing Physician. As a Flourishing Physician, you will take the steps that you need both to honor yourself, and to swing into action and move toward the life of your dreams. Two things are true: you are perfect just the way you are, and there are things about your life that you would like to change (as evidenced by the very fact that you are reading this). I want you to commit to yourself and decide right now. The more that you hesitate, the more that you procrastinate, the more that you waffle, the more time and the more power you are giving over to somebody else. I want you to stand up right now, and remember how much power that you have, and commit that you will use your power, your knowledge, your skills, your experiences–AND the tools in this book–to create the best life for yourself that you could ever imagine.

I'm so excited for you to take this journey with me. Let's dive right in.

My Story

About 10 years ago, I was in Amanda's shoes myself. I felt stuck, frustrated, and powerless. I had everything I had ever wanted when I was a child–a beautiful home, a wonderful daughter, work I enjoyed–and yet I was unfulfilled and restless. I had just been through a divorce from my daughter's father, and my entire world was turned upside down.

I didn't have clear boundaries for myself, and it led to challenges in all my relationships, including intimate, friend, and work-related relationships. I felt like the stress and bodily toll from my medical training were still having a negative impact on my health and well-being. I was surviving but not thriving. I had suppressed so many of my negative emotions over the years and didn't have the tools to work through them effectively, so they built up and created obstacles to my success. I saw so many others around me, seemingly fulfilled and truly happy, and I felt envious of them and wondered what their secret was. I had difficulty finding motivation to do even the things that I knew I enjoyed–spending time with friends, being out in nature, traveling, engaging in exciting work projects–and not doing things that I enjoyed only deepened my frustration.

Even though I loved my work and my colleagues, the ethos in my work environment was "get it done at all costs." I felt like I couldn't take time off. I knew of physicians who rolled their IV fluids into the exam rooms and gave themselves breathing treatments in between patients, just because they didn't feel they could go home when they were sick. (If there are any silver linings to the COVID-19 pandemic, one of them surely is the mindset of not going to work when you are sick.) My colleagues would frequently share with me that they took days off just to catch up on charting.

People were celebrated for working while on vacation. I can't count the number of meetings I attended–in person or virtual–where the "thank yous" echoed when someone said they were participating while off. There was an expectation to monitor emails while out or on weekends and holidays. Many times, I happened to see an early (pre-8 a.m.) Monday morning meeting invite that wasn't there the previous Friday at 5 p.m. All of this created an environment where there was no permission to be truly off.

At the time, it wasn't clear to me how harmful this environment was. I felt proud of my strong work ethic and proud of my accomplishments, so I stayed afloat by following the implicit rules of the game. I chalked up the inner tension I felt to the stress of the job and to being a busy physician and mom. **I didn't know that there was another way to be until I started working with a coach.**

I was assigned an executive coach as part of a cohort of physician leaders. I had never worked with a coach before and wasn't sure what to expect. During our first few sessions, I felt a sense of trust and safety, and I knew that our work together would be incredibly impactful to me both personally and professionally. As she got to know me, she sensed my frustration with my environment and she showed me that there was another path. There was another way of thinking, being, and acting in the world that would be more in alignment with my values.

I had so many fears getting in my way at the time. The fear of failure. The fear of rejection. The fear of the unknown. The fear of success (yes, this is real–it has to do with the fear that, if I'm successful, other people would have high expectations of me that I wouldn't be able to meet). I found it difficult to take risks and often preferred to stay safe, stay small, and keep the status quo rather than try anything new.

Working with my coach, I realized I had been allowing these fears to take control and inhibit my personal and professional growth. I had been trained in a culture that valued "coloring within the lines" and "staying in my lane." I feared that if I stepped outside the well-established boundaries that were pre-defined for me, I would lose everything and everyone that was important to me. I was worried I would lose my status as a physician leader and all the positional power and prestige I had worked so hard for.

My coach validated my fears and provided the psychological safety and encouragement to take small steps outside my comfort zone. She helped me see that I didn't have to feel so stuck. Not only did I not have to feel so stuck, but it was also imperative for my own well-being, and for everyone around me, that I get un-stuck. My own limiting beliefs, and the behaviors that followed, were, in fact, limiting my ability to serve others. Over the course of several years, I broke free of the constraints that were surrounding me and discovered a new way of living–a way that is in alignment with my values and with my true self.

The journey at times is difficult, but it has been the most rewarding experience of my life. I liken it to Dorothy's journey down the yellow brick road in *The Wizard of Oz* (one of my favorite movies as a child). Dorothy has a singular goal in mind–to make it to the Emerald City and ask the Wizard to send her home. Along the way, she encounters some dark characters, as well as more beauty than she could have ever imagined. She's guided by her mentor, Glinda, and supported by her friends Toto, Scarecrow, Tin Man, and Cowardly Lion. She knows she couldn't have made the journey without them, and she had to experience the whole gamut of emotions in order to arrive back home. That's why Glinda didn't tell her to click her heels at the beginning of the movie; as she said at the end, "You had to learn it for yourself." We don't learn passively, by reading or hearing–we learn through experience. Dorothy had to experience the journey for herself to fully realize "there's no place like home."

Just like Dorothy, I had to experience the journey for myself and learn along the way. The impact has been tremendous. I've been able to set and maintain boundaries for myself in every aspect of my life. In my personal life, as I was dating post-divorce, I became crystal clear on what I wanted and needed in a partner. I created a vision for my ideal future husband (knowing I wanted to get married again) and intentionally spent my time and energy with people who would move me closer to that vision. I'm a firm believer in the energy of the universe–that when we make an internal shift, everything around us shifts. This shift set the stage for my current husband to enter the picture again. (We had known each other tangentially, several years before we started dating.) He's encouraged and championed my personal and professional development in ways I couldn't have even imagined.

In my professional life, I realized my true calling was coaching. The process of coach training is an incredible growth opportunity. Learning "how to coach" is the tip of the iceberg. What's underneath the surface of the water are the internal mindset shifts that I've had to make in order to be an effective coach. My first and most important client is me. If I'm not walking the walk, I can't talk the talk. If I'm not prioritizing my own needs, managing my difficult emotions, and maintaining boundaries, I can't be an effective coach. I continue to work with a coach to be the best version of myself possible.

Soon after starting to coach, it was clear to me that my passion is to pursue coaching full-time. In 2021, I launched my business, **The Purposeful MD, with the mission of helping physicians to create the lives they love without guilt**. My own personal and professional growth allowed me to leave my corporate job and medical practice after 14 years to focus on my coaching business full-time. I don't believe I would have had the courage to do so if I hadn't been down this path of personal development, and if I didn't have the support of my coaches, my family, and my friends.

I also acknowledge the privileges with which I've been blessed throughout my life. I'm a cis, hetero, able-bodied white person. Those qualities with which I was born no doubt eliminated obstacles for me that so many others face. I must recognize my privilege, so that I'm not using it unfairly to my advantage, and advocate for equity so that everyone has access to the tools they need to succeed. I must also not minimize the challenges that I have faced and share my own story so that it may help someone else to not suffer.

Like Dorothy, my journey has been a mixture of pain and beauty. I can wholeheartedly, absolutely state that it has been 100% worth it in the end. I've brought myself into full alignment with my values and my true nature. I've surrounded myself with such an amazing cadre of coaches, friends, and champions, and I know that I am never alone. More than anything, I want this for you too.

Chapter 1
DEFINE YOUR WHY

"The future belongs to those who believe in the beauty of their dreams."
–Eleanor Roosevelt

When my daughter was just turning 6, I became a single parent. I use the term loosely, because my daughter's father and I share custody, and he has been and continues to be a very active parent. She spends every other week with me. After my divorce, I quickly had to adjust my priorities so that I could be most present for her when she was with me, and shift some of my other roles and duties to those time periods when she was with her dad.

At the same time, I was advancing rather quickly as a medical director in my organization. I also started an MBA program that I had committed to several months before my now ex-husband and I decided to separate. I loved my colleagues and the work I was doing.

As is true in many corporate environments, most of my professional colleagues were men. A majority of the men had wives that were stay-at-home parents. This meant that they didn't deal with many of the struggles that I did. They weren't the ones getting the call from day care to pick up a sick child. They didn't have to make sure they were home when the A/C repair company arrived. They didn't have to rush out of a meeting that's running long so they can pick up their child before day care closes. They didn't have to take time off for a veterinarian appointment to say goodbye to their beloved family pet.

It turns out this situation wasn't unique to me as a single parent. There were a few other women physicians around me who were rising or established leaders. I noticed that, in general, the ones who rose most quickly, and earned the coveted positions/titles/roles, were either childless or had older children (and therefore fewer or no childcare responsibilities). The women in my peer group who had small children had similar struggles related to caring for sick children, picking up children on time from school or day care, or fighting the guilt that came from "not having balance."

It didn't seem fair. I felt like I was being judged as a less committed employee because I was committed to being a good parent. I felt like I had to constantly defend my actions. I remember hearing an off-hand comment once, from a respected leader during a meeting, about single moms asking for special consideration (related to time off or a revised schedule) and how that didn't seem right. I immediately felt ashamed of my situation and felt that I was, and would always be, excluded from the "boys' club."

Impossible Expectations

It didn't seem fair, and it turns out that it isn't fair. As recently as 2020, Gallup data showed that women continue to shoulder the burden of childcare and household duties.

The COVID-19 pandemic highlighted the inequity, with a disproportionate percentage of women having left the workforce (and, as of 2022, not returned) to care for children or aging parents.

Women have made a great deal of progress over the past few decades, related to financial independence and advancement in the workplace. Our grandmothers, and maybe even mothers, couldn't take out a credit card unless they were married! What hasn't advanced, however, are gender roles in the home. Far more women than men stay home to care for children. Women tend to be responsible for most of the home-related upkeep. The systemic and cultural imbalance is still there. Look at any women's magazine and you'll see scores of articles discussing home decorating, cooking, and cleaning hacks, while men's magazines tend to be focused on health, sports, and hobbies.

This all adds up to expectations for women that are even more impossible to meet. We are expected to "lean in" in the workplace, and also maintain a spotless home with perfectly behaved children. The deck is still stacked against us. To complicate matters, we internalize these expectations because they are so ingrained in society, and because many of these expectations were modeled for us in our families of origin. The expectations are unrealistic, and yet both so commonplace and so strong, that we become overwhelmed when we can't meet them. We don't even see the expectations as out of whack.

Many of my female physician clients express frustration around the "second shift"–coming home in the evening after a long day of patient care/administrative work, and still being expected or feeling obligated to cook, clean, help with homework, get kids into bed, care for pets and/or extended family members, and a myriad of other duties. How many times do we hear a mother brag about her husband "helping with the kids"? He's not "helping" when they're his children too!

It's clear that we still have a long way to go. The systemic gender imbalance will take a long time to fix itself. As I watch my teenage daughter and young adult step-daughters assert themselves in the world in a way that makes me so proud, I have a great deal of hope that the tide is starting to turn. Young women are not accepting this current imbalance. As we see more diversity in family types–children raised by parents and other family members of various genders–the status quo may be turned completely upside down within a generation.

It can help to acknowledge the imbalance, as it stands

today-not so that we see ourselves as victims, but so that we can clearly see reality. If we acknowledge the environment, then we can begin to work with it in a way that is incredibly empowering. We can choose how we respond in any given situation. I love this quote by Victor Frankl, from his seminal work *Man's Search for Meaning*: "Everything can be taken from a man but one thing: the last of the human freedoms-to choose one's attitude in any given set of circumstances, to choose one's own way."

We have tremendous freedom that we may not even realize. We can make intentional choices about where we spend our time and our energy. We can define what's important in our own lives and what we will and will not tolerate. We can set boundaries that align with our core values. We can then unravel the expectations in our lives and environment and accept that there is some discomfort, especially in the beginning, as we prioritize ourselves and our needs. The payoff, however, is definitely worth it. Even more beautifully, as we do this work, we give permission to women all around us to set boundaries and unravel expectations for themselves. We break the mold so that the expectations are no longer there.

Where Time Management Fits In

One common struggle I hear from my physician coaching clients is wanting to improve their time management. As I mentioned before, time management encompasses so many different aspects of life. Because of my work with clients and with myself on time management, when I hear this from a client, I trust my inner knowing that something else is underlying this desire. When I begin to ask questions about this goal, I discover what's underneath–challenges with setting boundaries, managing strong emotions, and questioning ingrained beliefs–all surface as we work on the seemingly simple issue of time management.

When you think of time management–what comes to mind? Do you think of prioritization? Efficiency? Getting things done? Doing the "hard stuff" first? Doing things that you don't want to do (like doing your homework before you went out to play as a kid)?

You may think that time management is dry and boring; "managed time" means you can't have any fun. You may be judging yourself for how you've managed your time in the past. Remember, you've clearly demonstrated a near superhuman capacity to discipline yourself and manage your time to make it where you are in life! You may also be thinking, "If I could only manage my time better, my life would be so much easier!"

This may be true. However, "time management" is only part of the story. It's helpful here to take a step back and define what time management means for the purposes of this book. We may have been socialized to think of time management as increasing our productivity. My argument against that definition is that the word "productivity" implies that we are only as valuable as what we produce. It leaves out the inherent value of things like rest and play (which we will explore later in the book).

My definition of time management is *the act of being intentional and purposeful about where and how you spend your time and energy.*

You have the power to decide where and how your time and energy are spent. You're in the drivers' seat–and you don't give up the wheel to anyone else.

For us to truly manage our time better, we must confront some beliefs and ideas that we may have held our whole lives. It's not as simple as just using techniques you may have read about or tried, such as time blocking or productivity hacks. While some of these things can help, unless we address the underlying beliefs that we've held for so long about ourselves and our expectations, these hacks will fail. We will encounter resistance, because we are coming up against our ego, which wants to keep us safe and prevent us from taking risks. However, you can–and you WILL–overcome your ego!

A client recently came to me asking for help with managing her time better. This happens frequently, and usually the client is expecting me to give them tips and tricks on how to be more efficient or get things done more quickly. There's nothing inherently wrong with this approach, but it doesn't lead to long-lasting change. As I mentioned before, hacks will only get you so far. Think about how often our patients heed our well-intended advice to follow their prescribed eating plan or exercise program–not as often as we would like. It's critical that we break down the process into steps, so that we can create new neural pathways which lead to sustainable behavior changes and the results that we want.

The first question I asked my client was, "On a scale of 1-10, 1 being not important at all, and 10 being incredibly important and your life depends on it, how important is it for you to manage your time better?" She rated it an 8. That's a great place to be–anywhere 7 or higher is most helpful. If the end state isn't important to us, we won't stick with it when the going gets tough. If she had said 6 or less, I would have suggested that she choose another goal for our coaching conversation that day.

My next question was, "**Why** is this important to you?" She had to stop and think; she thought this would have been obvious to me. Of COURSE she wants to manage her time better… doesn't everyone? Her answer was, "I want to spend more time with my son." I asked her to be more specific, and she said she wanted to focus on being with her young son, and doing an activity of his choosing in the evenings after dinner. She had been longing to do this but was often catching up on charts in the evenings, or she was so distracted by everything she had to do that she wasn't being fully present with him. Either way, she was feeling incredibly guilty. Together, we created a plan (utilizing the methods outlined in this book) that was doable for her to create more quality time with her son.

If we don't have a strong purpose–a strong "why" for doing something–we will find it difficult or impossible to sustain the behavior, even if the behavior is something we want to do! Being clear on our *why* will focus our attention and remind us of the reason we are changing. Change is hard, and remembering our purpose can nudge us in the direction we want to go. (Sometimes it's more of a shove than a nudge!)

How does all of this relate to time management?

If we aren't clear on our "why," we expend time and energy on things that aren't important to us. We give away our time and our power to other people's priorities. Since we don't have endless time and energy, we don't allow ourselves the space to create what we truly want in our lives. We waste precious time and energy on activities and people that don't bring us joy and don't light us up, leaving less time and energy for the activities and people that allow us to be our best selves.

Action Step

Grab your journal and a pen and let's get into action. You can also reference the Purposeful MD downloadable journal (https://thepurposefulmd.com/book).

- Pick a behavior that you want to start (or stop) doing. Choose something that's been slightly difficult for you in the past, but not so difficult that your body shuts down

or becomes hyperactivated when you think about it. Write down this behavior (or stopping of the behavior).
- How important is this to you, on a scale of 1-10 (1 being not at all important, and 10 being very important)? Write down your number. If your number is 7 or greater, stick with this behavior. If your number is 6 or less, choose another one that's 7 or greater.
- What's your "why" for changing? Be as specific as possible. Imagine a new future with you having changed your behavior in this way. Write down your "why" and as many details as you can for your new and improved future.

As a reminder, action is where the magic happens! For years, I consumed so much information in the form of books and yet wondered why nothing was changing in my life. I was learning so many new amazing concepts! Why wasn't my learning translating into anything different?

The answer? Because I wasn't acting on the new information. Action is NECESSARY for forward motion, for any change in your life. Remember–if nothing changes, nothing changes! Commit to yourself that you will put these concepts into action. You deserve it and you're worth it... you're a Flourishing Physician!

As a Flourishing Physician, you:

- Acknowledge the inherent biases that are present in society and especially in the medical community.
- Understand that you are NOT alone.
- Are ready and willing to do the work to get unstuck.
- Are clear on your "why" for making a change.
- Take action on your insights!

Further Reading

https://news.gallup.com/poll/283979/women-handle-main-household-tasks.aspx

https://www.uschamber.com/workforce/data-deep-dive-a-decline-of-women-in-the-workforce

Chapter 2
CLARIFY YOUR GOALS

"It takes as much energy to wish as it does to plan."
–Eleanor Roosevelt

I started running half-marathons in 2012. The impetus first came from wanting to increase my physical activity after my daughter was born, then watching friends and colleagues take up distance running, then deciding that I was up for the challenge. I'll admit there was a component of "take that!" aimed at my gym teacher who made fun of my running form in middle school. I hated running as a kid; in high school, it was actually a form of punishment (we had to run laps if we arrived late to marching band practice).

I began running consistently when my daughter was a baby. We purchased a jogging stroller and she loved being in it so much. I would take her after work while my then-husband, who had been staying home with her all day, prepared dinner. It was a win-win-win for all of us. My daughter loved being in the stroller and feeling the breeze in her face, I got in some exercise, and my husband enjoyed the empty house for half an hour so he could cook without distractions.

As I developed the habit of running and began signing up for races (mostly short fun runs, followed soon after by my first half-marathon), I realized how much I appreciated the idea of training for races and the gift of the goal at the end of the training cycle. Knowing the goal allowed me to break the training plan down into smaller components. As much as I loved running for running's sake (I wasn't trying to hit any time or pace goals during the races), I always preferred to have a race on the calendar so that I had a clear outcome to aim for. Stephen Covey famously stated, "Begin with the end in mind," and that concept felt so helpful for me throughout my training process. The race day goal created a container for me in which I could clearly and easily know whether I was on or off track with my training plan. Having money invested in the endeavor–the cost of the race, the training plan, and the coach– also helped me to commit and meet my goal.

When I started training for my first half-marathon, I had never run more than 4 miles at a time. Each long run was a new milestone for me, and a new opportunity to celebrate (which I often did not do at the time–more on celebration later in the book!). Finishing my first half-marathon was a huge accomplishment. If you've ever done anything similar, you know that the accomplishment isn't so much in the race itself–

it's in everything leading up to the race. The training, the miles, the sweat, the pain, the waking up early, the discipline, the saying "no" to happy hours and/or ice cream, the dedication to the literal and figurative path…for me, running has become a metaphor for life.

Clarifying the Goal

One concept I learned throughout the process is the importance of clarifying my goals–being crystal clear on what I want to happen. It would have been impossible for me to begin half-marathon training by saying "I'm going to run more over the next few months." What does that mean, exactly? How would I know if I have accomplished that goal?

If I didn't want to end up in the medical tent halfway through the race, I needed to be more specific with my training plan. There needed to be an objective measurement of whether I achieved my weekly running goal. Each iteration became more clear; the next was, "I need to run 4 times per week." This is much clearer, but I needed to go further, to how long or far each run needed to be, knowing that running for 5 minutes 4 times per week is vastly different than running for 30 minutes 4 times per week. I also needed to decide what type of running would be involved in each workout: running hills vs. flat, sprints vs. slow pace, etc. Not only that, I also had to factor in rest days, my work schedule, prior commitments, family obligations, and the like. Working along with my running coach and training group, I settled on a training plan that was clear, objective, and realistic, then put it all on a monthly calendar noting the length and pace of each run.

Often when we set a goal, it is so vague that it's not helpful. Vague goals are difficult for our brains to visualize, and our brains don't want to do anything difficult. We are wired for simplicity, so when we think of something difficult (even subconsciously), we encounter a huge amount of resistance. We can't progress toward vague or unclear goals, so we typically stop trying. This leaves us even more frustrated because we aren't working toward something that we seemingly truly want. Vague goals cause our brains to spend unnecessary time and energy deciding whether we've completed it. As a result, we exhaust ourselves just thinking about it, and then we avoid thinking about it because it's too exhausting. But if it *is* something we really want, our brains keep reminding us of the goal AND the fact that we aren't hitting it, adding to the frustration and feeling of failure. We're frustrated because we aren't achieving our goals, and then criticizing ourselves on top of the frustration. It's a recipe for disaster!

If we set a goal that turns out to be something we truly want, then why do we struggle so much to work effectively toward that goal?

Goals can be very scary, especially for high-achieving physicians. One reason for this is the fear of failure. For example, a physician may really want to make $500,000 of revenue in a year, but may fear setting that as a goal. There is a voice inside of her that says, "If you set that goal and you don't achieve it, you will have failed." She may then justify lowering her expectations to avoid feeling that she has failed. We are trained in a culture that tells us, "Failure is not an option," and to avoid failure at all costs. What we must do is redefine what "failure" means by clarifying our goals and redefining success.

I've seen this frequently in physicians I have coached. What can be helpful is a gentle reminder that the goal is arbitrary. That doesn't mean the goal isn't real or important to them, but *they* are the ones who set the goal. The goal is set by internal rather than external standards. We then ask: what was the purpose of setting this goal? Another way of asking this is: what's the goal *behind* the goal?

In the example above, the goal *behind* the goal of making $500,000 in revenue in a year could be to increase the efficiency of her clinic operation, to increase her patient panel, and/or to add more services for her current patient population. The $500,000 target is a nice outcome to expect from those above activities. However, there may be many factors outside of her control, related to revenue generation (staffing, billing, coding challenges, among others) that the goal itself is daunting. What if the goal was shifted to increasing her patient panel? This is a much more realistic and achievable goal and is directly within her control and influence.

Now that we've clarified the goal, we can begin to identify

what needs to happen to reach the goal. This is another area that often trips up physicians. We tend to think that "massive action" is required to meet the goal. "I need to attend a marketing event and sign up 200 patients in one afternoon!" That's another reason why the goals can seem daunting. It would be great if we could take huge leaps at a time toward our goals; while this does occasionally happen, most goals are achieved through small, consistent action. Olympic athletes are created from daily exercise and sustained habits, not through massive leaps and feats of greatness.

One of my clients, a highly successful, high-achieving nurse practitioner, told me that her goal was to leave her office at the end of a workday feeling "done" for the day. She wanted to feel accomplished both at work and at home, but she felt like she could never catch up with everything that has to get "done." She was constantly frustrated and felt guilty because she always felt her work was unfinished when she went home. She carried that guilt home with her to her family, where she spent her evenings catching up on patient charts after her kids went to bed. She wished she could spend more time with her husband, have time for herself, and exercise 3 times a week… but felt she could not carve out the time to do so. Her words to me were, "I feel like I'm always behind no matter what I do."

My first question to her was, "What does it mean for you to be 'done' for the day?"

She paused because she hadn't really considered that

question. She just knew she felt perpetually behind, and those feelings were bringing her close to burnout and close to leaving clinical practice, despite her love for teaching and patient care.

We spent most of that coaching conversation creating a definition of "done" for her. Until she had defined it clearly in her mind, she constantly felt like she was failing to meet her own expectations…but she didn't know what those expectations were! She felt that she was failing at a game without knowing the rules.

Her first definition of "done" was, "I've completed all my charts from today's visits and answered all incoming patient-related messages." Her goal was very clear, and creating the goal led to a sense of relief that I could perceive via our Zoom call. Now, her brain would not be constantly deciding what the goal is, and then calculating whether she had completed it.

Knowing her workload, my second question to her was, "Is that a realistic goal?" If the goal is not realistic, our brains will quickly realize that it's too difficult to achieve from the outset, and we will encounter resistance. Once again, the resistance, and the guilt that likely follows, will cause us to feel that we have failed.

She paused for another moment, smiled, and said, "It's probably not realistic." The goal was aspirational for her–she felt it was a goal she "should" be meeting–but it just wasn't feasible for her at this stage of her life. I then asked her, "What does it feel like in your body, when you think of hitting this goal every day?" My point here was to begin to make the connection between her bodily sensations and her emotions. We know how much wisdom our bodies hold; often, our bodies know something before our minds do. Zeroing in on the sensations in the body can be the key to better recognizing, understanding, and working with our emotions. (More on strong emotions later in the book!)

She said, "It feels tight and anxious." That's not a great starting place–we will subconsciously move away from these sensations–so her body could be fighting against her desire to achieve her goal. This is a form of self-sabotage that can make it difficult for us to change anything, even if it's a change we really want to make! Part of what led to her anxiety was that her goal was dependent on the behaviors of other people. In this example, her behavior was dependent on her clinical staff not sending her urgent messages late in the day. It's important that our goals be under our complete control and not dependent on what someone else does or doesn't do. Holding onto a goal that is dependent on someone else will cause our brains to scream, "Danger!" and lead to resistance, in the same way that an unclear or vague goal does.

I asked her to imagine a more realistic goal and then check in with her body. Her next stated goal was to leave work at 5:30 p.m. with fewer than 5 open charts and 5 unread inbox messages. She said this goal felt more open and at ease, almost relaxing, in her body. This is a great place to be, because those feelings are pleasurable, and our bodies will move toward them. Her new goal was straightforward, realistic, and fully within her control. Once she had landed on her goal, I asked her to write it down in specific detail, so that it became clearer and more cemented in her mind. We then crafted a plan to batch her tasks throughout the day to meet this goal, creating new, small, manageable habits during the day to ensure she hit her targets.

Another physician client of mine asked for help with his goal to "get in shape" (his words). He was struggling to get started and, as an accomplished physician leader, was frustrated for several reasons. First, he had been an avid exerciser years ago and truly enjoyed it, so the absence was notable to him. Second, he knew how important exercise was to his overall physical and mental health. He said he felt like an "imposter" counseling his patients to exercise when he wasn't participating himself.

I acknowledged and honored his frustration and assured him he was not alone. The first step was to clarify what he meant by "get in shape." He said he wanted to begin a regular exercise routine. I asked him why this was important to him; he replied that heart disease ran in his family and he wanted to reduce his risk. He also wanted to lose some weight that he had gained over the past year. I validated his clear "why" as this will help propel him forward.

I then asked him to clarify even further. What type of exercise? When will he do this? Where will he do this? How often and for how long? What is his contingency when barriers arise? His role required frequent evening meetings, and he needed a backup plan if he was asked to attend a meeting that conflicted with a planned workout.

We spent the rest of the session crafting a fool-proof plan that he could follow. At our next session two weeks later, he shared his success. He had been able to stick to the plan easily and he was feeling so much more confident as a result. (We will discuss confidence later in the book. Spoiler alert: confidence comes from taking action, not the other way around.)

How does all of this relate to time management?

With a clear goal and a defined plan, we can decide once upfront what we will do, and we don't have to decide each time we start to take action. In the example above, with my client creating an exercise plan, he didn't have to decide every day, "Am I going to exercise? What type of exercise am I going to do? For how long will I exercise? Where will I exercise?" He created the plan once, and all he had to do was execute. He also didn't have to negotiate with himself; he had already decided. He also created some flexibility for himself…if he had planned for an evening workout, and was asked to attend a work-related dinner, his backup plan was to work out the following morning instead. He anticipated possible barriers and planned for them in advance. He reduced the friction points beforehand, which allowed him to be more successful. This one habit helped him to plan more effectively in other areas of his life, improving his overall time management skills.

Action Step

Grab your journal and a pen and let's get into action. You can also reference the Purposeful MD downloadable journal (https://thepurposefulmd.com/book).

1. Review the behavior you wrote down in Chapter 1 that you want to start or stop doing. Write down a goal related to this behavior change that you'd like to set for yourself.
2. Re-read your goal. Is it specific enough? Could a kindergartner watch you do the behavior, and determine whether or not you completed it? (It's "drink 32 ounces of water every day before 3 p.m." vs "drink more water.")
3. Is the goal realistic?
    a. Put down your pen and close your eyes for a moment. Picture yourself taking the steps needed to accomplish your goal.
    b. What do you notice in your body? Do any areas of your body tighten up or tense up…or do you notice your body beginning to relax and settle into the moment?
    c. If you notice tensing or tightening, re-write your goal to make it less challenging and more doable. Repeat step 3 until you feel the sense of ease and peace in your body.
4. Is the goal completely within your control? If not, re-

write the goal including only those behaviors that are 100% within your control-that you can do regardless of the actions of anyone else (or worse, things completely out of our control, such as the weather).
5. Create a doable plan to meet this goal, answering the questions of when, where, how, and what you will do when barriers arise.

Remember, goals can change. Once you meet your desired goal, you can always adjust and move the goalpost. Pick something doable that you can and will accomplish-this will help develop more confidence and propel you to take even more action in the future!

As a Flourishing Physician, you...

- Understand the importance of clarifying your goals.
- Define exactly what needs to happen-what YOU need to do-to reach the goal.
- Only focus on goals that are 100% in your control.
- Know how it feels in your body when your goals are realistic and doable.
- Take action on your insights!

Chapter 3
OUTSMART YOUR SNEAKY BRAIN

"You can often change your circumstances by changing your attitude."
–Eleanor Roosevelt

In 2022, my family and I moved into a different house about 10 minutes away from where we were currently living. Even though the home was about the same size as our current home, we were downsizing from five bedrooms to three. Packing and moving required a significant amount of decluttering and deciding what to sell or donate. Throughout the entire process, I often felt overwhelmed with STUFF. It made me feel like I had lost control (even the word "stuff" sounds awful). I typically prefer a calm, orderly setting, and the chaotic physical environment caused quite a bit of anxiety for me.

The anxiety was unsettling. I was so excited to move into

our new home, which fit our family more perfectly, and yet I couldn't shake the stress in the process. By working with my business coach, taking quiet reflection time, and journaling, I realized that my anxious feelings were a direct result of my thoughts about the situation. My thoughts about my "stuff" led to a feeling that I had lost control. This feeling made me feel inherently unsafe and scared. So, my brain convinced me to do ANYTHING to regain a sense of control: checking and rechecking to-do lists, micromanaging my family's packing process, and more...none of which assuaged my anxiety. In fact, my stress worsened (as did the stress of my family members too!).

Have you ever had an intense desire to clean when you were anxious? That's your brain trying to grab onto control! It's a normal and human response which can sometimes help us process overwhelm or trauma. When I was studying for my MBA, I clearly remember sitting in my comfy leather chair, curled up with a book and my dog in my lap. I knew that I needed to study for my exam the following day, but my brain convinced me that that exact moment was the *perfect* time to clean out the refrigerator. I'm telling you, my refrigerator and my closets have never been as clean and organized as when I was studying for my masters' classes!

With the support of my coach, I was able to re-frame the thoughts about the moving process so they did not provoke anxiety. I realized that I could choose to view the clutter as suffocating or as freeing: as a symbol of my values, a representation of who I am now and who I am becoming, a sign of the many blessings life has bestowed upon me, and as a reminder of how excited I am to be building a life and creating new memories with my family in our beautiful new home.

All the objects–the *stuff*–represented my memories, my journey, my life, my joys and setbacks, and the love I share with my family and friends.

I can choose the thoughts that persist. I can assign meaning to the STUFF and what it represents. I can decide which thoughts hold power over me: those that create overwhelm, or those that create freedom.

The Power of Thoughts

Our thoughts hold a great amount of power over us. In any given situation, our thoughts can lead directly to our feelings about that situation and can also drive our behaviors. In my example above, my thoughts about my clutter and moving boxes initially caused me to feel anxious. I resisted the uncomfortable, anxious feelings and asked my coach for support to manage them; her response was to help me reframe the thoughts so that I felt gratitude rather than anxiety. I was able to consciously choose to think, "These boxes mean I've been fortunate to have all the things I need and I'm grateful to be moving into a new home," instead of, "This stuff is driving me crazy, and I wish someone else would deal with it."

Our thoughts have even more power over us than just our feelings. There's a great model, conceived by Larry Senn of Senn Delaney Leadership Consulting, called "the results cone." This model states that our thoughts directly lead to our behaviors, which then directly lead to our results. If we examine the concept backwards, to change our results, we must change our behaviors, which requires changing our thoughts. Changing behavior is difficult; you know this if you have ever tried to begin a new habit or break an old one. We can change our behavior in the short term without changing our thoughts, but our egos will often rebel unless we develop new thought habits.

Let's use an example. Imagine that you are a primary care physician with a patient panel of 5,000 patients and you want to increase your panel to 7,500. Your current results are the panel size of 5,000 patients. There could be many behaviors (or absence of behaviors) that led to those results: not asking for patient referrals, allowing your staff to schedule new patients several months out rather than within a few weeks, and not advertising your clinic and services. Your thoughts may be, "My patients will get offended if I ask them for a referral," or, "I can't schedule my new patients any sooner than I currently am," or, "I don't have the money to hire a marketing team." Continuing to think those thoughts will lead to the same behaviors (or absence of behaviors). You may try a new behavior for a short period of time, but you won't be able to sustain it, because without shifting your thinking, your brain will rebel against the new behavior.

What if you chose a new thought…a thought that moves you closer to the behavior you want to take and closer to the desired results–a panel size of 7,500 patients? Examples of more helpful thoughts may be: "My patients would be glad to refer a friend or family member to me," or, "I can make time for a new patient once or twice a week," or, "I can look for cost-effective marketing resources to help with advertising." These thoughts open the door to new behaviors that will then lead you to your desired results.

The new thoughts often create very doable and achievable behaviors. If the behaviors seem just as daunting as the original goal, they are not likely to be sustained. The behaviors have to be simple to allow for healthy habits to form. Again, small consistent daily actions are the keys here; we are not waiting for or hoping for "massive action" to occur because massive action is not necessary. As author James Clear says in his book *Atomic Habits*, "Every action you take is a vote for the type of person you wish to become." Thoughts are the gateway to creating sustainable actions.

As you begin to practice noticing your thoughts, and experimenting with new ones that lead to different behaviors (and better results), you will likely feel some internal conflict. Your new thoughts may conflict with belief systems that you learned as a child or young adult. These thoughts may have served you well in the past but are not serving you at this stage of your life. You will come up against strong emotions and we will discuss how to work through those in Chapter 6.

If you're like me, a common thought starts with the phrase, "I should." There are so many reasons that we use the word "should." Many of them stem from expectations placed on us by society, our families, our work environments, and social media, just to name a few. I hear this frequently in my coaching clients, and I mention it when I hear them use the phrase. I will lovingly ask them to "stop shoulding all over themselves." The word "should" carries a lot of weight and often reveals that we are burdening ourselves with someone else's expectations. We can instead choose a new thought, which may mean "I want to" or, "I will" or, in the negative, "I don't want to" or, "I won't." Simply rephrasing the thought in a different way is tremendously empowering.

Recently I was coaching a clinician who told me she wants to finish reading a book to feel a sense of accomplishment. She said to me, "I start things and then I don't finish them." As a good coach...I had a hunch that wasn't completely true. I recognized this as a thought that was leading to a negative feeling of self-doubt. In order to challenge that thought, I asked her about times in her life when she HAS finished something that she started, and she named several. I added several more–including her medical training–for which she wasn't crediting herself.

She had a pervasive thought that wasn't serving her. This

happens ALL THE TIME.

We questioned the thought together and explored whether there was a better thought that would lead her to a more productive feeling. The thought she picked that empowered her and served her more effectively was, "I finish what I set my mind to do." She left the coaching session feeling more confident and accomplished.

Have you ever had a thought like…

I want to (insert goal)…but I don't have the time.

I wish I could pick up my hobby again.

After my kids are older, I'll have time for…

Everyone else has resources to do what they want to do, but not me.

How do those thoughts make you feel? Possibly hopeless or despondent?

What if we didn't have to think those thoughts? What if we actively reframed those thoughts into ones that will actually change how you feel, and even more powerfully, propel you forward?

Let's experiment with a new set of thoughts, such as:

I'll make the time for what's important.

I can do what I want to do NOW.

I deserve to prioritize what's important to me.

How do those thoughts make you feel? WORTHY, VALUED, PRODUCTIVE.

Practicing this technique has been one of the most powerful tools in my toolbelt.

One of my coaching clients, a very driven and successful nurse practitioner, shared with me during a recent session that she had an insight in the weeks since our previous session. The goal that she had been working on was not charting past 10 p.m. during the week so that she could prioritize sleep. During our third or fourth session, she said she had been consistent with this action and she noticed how much more energy she had, since she was getting a full night's sleep most nights. During our fifth session, she shared with me that, in the previous week, one of her clinical colleagues was out sick. In addition to covering for her colleague, she was asked to join a new committee and was invited to the weekly meetings, further cutting into her time to catch up on charting. She said she "fell back into bad habits" and stayed up past 10 p.m. to finish her charts.

What she shared with me after describing this change of events was really powerful. She said that, "I felt myself slipping back," but that, because of our work together and practicing noticing her thoughts, instead of obsessing about the setback, and beating herself up, she saw this as an opportunity to grow and learn, and to realize that she truly does need to rest and sleep. She told me, "After I realized how important rest is, I got the rest I needed and now I feel so much better." She told herself, "It's not a setback. This is all part of the process. My week wasn't as bad as my brain told me it was."

She was able to reframe her thoughts in an empowering

way, and doing so allowed her to adjust her behavior much more quickly than if she had stayed in a negative thought pattern ("I failed, I messed up, I can't do this"). Her thoughts were creating her environment and creating the container for her to either grow or stay stuck. The reframe that she offered herself served her so much better.

A coach mentor of mine frequently would say, "Energy goes where attention flows." Our minds like to gravitate toward the negative. It's an evolutionary trait that allows us to quickly scan the environment and assess any potential threats or risks. However, we can redirect our energy here too, by intentionally choosing to focus on what we CAN do instead of what we CAN'T.

I've recently begun running again after a long absence. It's easy for me to focus on what I CAN'T do–as in, what I used to be able to do–so I must actively concentrate on what I CAN do. I may not be as fast as I was 5 years ago, but I can do my very best every day with the resources I have. The important thing is that I'm out there and enjoying the journey. My running coach is phenomenal about reminding me to focus on what I am able to do, so that my energy isn't wasted worrying about what I *used* to be able to do. Thinking in this way is incredibly empowering and opens my mind to so many more possibilities. I'm also able to be more grateful for the process and be compassionate to myself along the way (concepts we will explore later in the book).

How does all of this relate to time management?

When we are stuck in negative thought patterns, we allow ourselves to believe the stories our brains are telling us. We waste time and energy believing these stories, which are time and energy that could be better spent on activities or with people that we truly enjoy and that light us up. We can't be intentional about how we spend our time unless we challenge the negative thought patterns that lead to negative emotions and undesirable behaviors.

Action Step

Grab your journal and a pen and let's get into action. You can also reference the Purposeful MD downloadable journal (https://thepurposefulmd.com/book).

- Think of a situation that is causing you some discomfort. Start with something causing only a small amount of discomfort, rather than something incredibly stressful.
- As you think about this situation, your brain will be creating a ton of thoughts about it.
- Write down every single thought that comes to mind. Do not edit as you go. Do not judge your thoughts. Write down every single one.
- Keep writing until you have written every thought that comes to mind. This may take you at least 1-2 full pages.
- For each thought, ask yourself if that thought is serving you–leading to positive feelings–or if it's hindering you,

leading to negative feelings.
- For each thought that is hindering you, craft a different thought that will lead to better feelings. It's OK if the thought you craft isn't something that you entirely believe yet. Just write it down and notice what comes up when you do.
- Pick a few positive thoughts that resonate with you, and practice intentionally saying them to yourself when this situation arises. Again, it's OK if you don't believe them. Saying them to yourself helps train your brain to focus on more positive thoughts.
- Begin to notice in everyday life if your thoughts are serving you, or hindering you, and practice reframing the thoughts that aren't serving you into more powerful ones.

After you gain some practice noticing your thoughts and intentionally choosing kinder ones, you will notice powerful emotions arise–and we will work with these in Chapter 6.

As a Flourishing Physician, you...

- Recognize the thoughts that aren't serving you and that are leading to unpleasant emotions.
- Understand that your thoughts and emotions about a situation directly impact your behavior, which directly impacts your results.
- Question the thoughts that aren't serving you–ask yourself if they are really true.
- Choose different thoughts that lead to more productive emotions and behavior.
- Take action on your insights!

Chapter 4
TAKE A SMALL STEP

"We do not have to become heroes overnight. Just a step at a time, meeting each thing that comes up, seeing it as not as dreadful as it appears, discovering that we have the strength to stare it down."
–Eleanor Roosevelt

As I was writing this book, our world was slowly coming out of the COVID-19 pandemic, and many of us were reclaiming or rediscovering our lives and our purpose. During the pandemic years, I was running very infrequently for various reasons: stress from the pandemic itself, long work hours, the inability to run with others in groups (a huge pick-me-up), grief over losing my father in 2020, and the build-up of injuries. I realize now that all of these reasons were related; the stress and grief intensified my injuries, and that triad of issues made it difficult for me to run. Running is an outlet for me and is the best stress relief I've found, so not being able to run further intensified my stress and grief. It was a vicious cycle.

At the end of 2022, I decided "enough was enough." I decided to get back into serious training and signed up for both a 10k and a sprint triathlon (a short course race that includes swimming, biking, and running). Having not one but two races on the upcoming calendar spurred me into action. I also enlisted the support of a running coach to create a "return to running" training plan.

My initial excitement wore off once I realized, rather quickly, that my injuries didn't just disappear because I wanted them to, or because I didn't run for months at a time. I couldn't run 15 minutes without pain. As a distance runner, I know that some pain can accompany running, especially when increasing speed or mileage, but this was pain I couldn't keep ignoring.

I knew I needed additional help, so I scheduled a physical therapy evaluation. My therapist was amazing and applauded my goal of running pain-free (when my previous therapist repeatedly tried to convince me to stop running because of the "impact on my knees"). He prescribed a set of daily exercises that would improve my strength and mobility and decrease my pain.

Anyone who has ever done a recovery program like this knows that the hardest part is at the beginning. The exercise routine is tiring, often painful, and yields slow results. It also seemed so simple to me. My brain repeatedly told me, "There's no way that this simple leg lift you are doing is helping you toward your goal." I struggled with finding the motivation to do my exercises every day. What initially sparked me to do them was the respect and faith I had in my therapist, and not wanting to let him down.

I worked with my business coach to uncover the thoughts behind my resistance to the daily exercises. I KNEW they were intended to increase my strength, decrease my chance of further injury, and move me closer to my goal of running pain-free. Yet, some voice inside me chirped loudly enough, "You don't need to do those. Your exercises won't help. You'll get better on your own."

I began to ask myself why I wasn't motivated, and how I could *get* motivated to consistently do the exercises as prescribed. My coach lovingly said something to the effect of, "Motivation doesn't just fall out of the sky and land in your lap."

I had been waiting for motivation to hit me like a bolt of lightning. I then realized I had to either motivate myself, or not rely on motivation to act.

Lack of motivation can cause us to feel really stuck. When we feel stuck, our motivation wanes even more, decreasing even further, in a vicious cycle that is difficult to break on our own.

Working more with my coach, I began to explore the notion of motivation, and asked myself what it means to be motivated: that I *want* to do something? That I *need* to do something? That I *should* do something? That someone is telling me to do something?

I noticed that every single time I told myself, "I'm not motivated to do my physical therapy exercises," I felt more stuck. It felt like a dead end. I wasn't taking any action, and stringing together days of inaction worsened my injuries even more.

The Myth of Motivation

Motivation is fickle. We do tons of things throughout the day despite a perceived lack of "motivation." How often are you really, truly motivated to brush your teeth? But you (hopefully) do this every day, anyway. So what purpose does "motivation" really serve?

If I waited to feel motivated to do ANYTHING, I would be waiting a long, long time. If I kept waiting to feel "motivated" to do my P.T. exercises, I would never have done them.

I realized that either I needed to create my own motivation, or I needed to act despite not being motivated. Motivation was neither the silver bullet nor the secret ingredient to me getting the results I wanted.

One day I asked myself, "What if I do the exercises even though I'm not motivated?" I did the exercises and committed to doing them for several days in a row. Lo and behold, my running improved and my pain decreased. I realized that motivation wasn't necessary for me to be successful; *I just needed to take action.* Because it was *action* that was moving me closer to my goal–running pain-free. I felt empowered that I could take action without waiting for "motivation to fall into my lap."

We may not "be motivated" because it's an activity that carries a large amount of societal pressure. If we feel we are "supposed" to wake up early and work out (because that's what the "gurus" say), when we would prefer to work out in the evening (because that's easier on our bodies and our schedule), we may cloak that resistance as lack of motivation, when really, it's just not the right fit for us.

We also often tell ourselves we're "not motivated" because the task in front of us is too vague or undefined for our brains to process in the moment. We will go to many lengths and create all kinds of stories to avoid thinking about anything unclear. It's difficult to take action on a vague task because we don't know where to start. The more clearly we can define and clarify our actions, the more likely we are to take action.

One helpful distinction to break through the motivation barrier is understanding the difference between a task and a project. Many of us keep "task lists" that are actually "project lists." A task is one simple step; a project is anything made up of 3 or more tasks.

One of my physician clients was dealing with a difficult interpersonal situation. Throughout our session, it became clear to her that she was going to have to initiate an honest yet challenging conversation with her supervisor. Once she stated the need for this conversation and felt confident about what she wanted to say, as well as her desired outcome, I asked her a powerful question that I ask many of my clients when they are planning to take action: "What's the next step?"

She said, "I'm going to talk to my supervisor." I validated her initiative and her upcoming plan, then realized that the answer she had given me was actually a project containing multiple tasks. If she was unclear about exactly what she needed to do next, she would very likely, and unconsciously, avoid taking action. I asked her again, "What's the very next step?"

She paused for a moment, and said, "I'm going to send a calendar invite to my supervisor." This is much clearer, but still technically a project, as it involves opening her electronic calendar, finding an open hour, creating a calendar invite, and sending it to her supervisor (4 steps). Those steps can be completed very quickly, but they are each still distinct steps, which we discussed together. Now that she knew the very next step for her was to open her electronic calendar, the entire project of talking with her supervisor seemed less daunting, and her anxiety was greatly reduced.

I then asked her when she was going to do each of these steps, and since we had a few minutes left on the call, she completed the calendar invite while we were on the call together. If we hadn't been able to, I would have asked her to commit to a time to complete it and add it to her own calendar if necessary.

Breaking down projects into smaller tasks has massively reduced my stress when I look at my task list. Even if I don't break down the projects into smaller tasks right away, I write down the very next step that I need to take for each project.

Once that step is completed, I often find that I finish the project since I've got some momentum. Then I don't have to rely on motivation, and I don't waste a ton of mental energy mulling over what needs to happen next.

Adding tasks to my calendar has been a crucial step in my task management process. Ever since college, when I felt like I was managing multiple spinning plates (classes, extracurricular activities, work, social and family events), my calendar has been an organizational must for me. I don't have to try and remember everything; I add it to the calendar, and as long as I'm committing to a regular calendar review, I accomplish tasks with much more ease. I review my calendar monthly, weekly, and daily now, and I've reduced so much of the friction and stress that comes from "trying to keep everything straight." One of my physician clients titled the appointments on her calendar "meeting with myself" and she stuck to these just as if she had a meeting with an important leader (which is true–the leader was her!).

When getting started with a calendar, the big question is digital or paper. I highly recommend a digital calendar that is synced to both tasks and your email. The more you leverage technology to work for you–to add reminders and appointments–the less weight you will feel trying to remember everything yourself. Break free from the sticky note system and start using your digital calendar now to free up mental space. If it's not written down or typed in somewhere, it's not likely to get done.

How does all of this relate to time management?

Once our projects and tasks are more clearly defined, we can execute them much more quickly. This is even more effortless when we add projects and tasks to our calendar. We spend less time and energy making decisions on where to focus next. We've already outlined it and now we just have to act, and we are acting in alignment with our intentions and with our true purpose. And we aren't wasting time and energy waiting for motivation to push us in the right direction!

Action Step

Grab your journal and a pen and let's get into action. You can also reference the Purposeful MD downloadable journal (https://thepurposefulmd.com/book).

- First, do a "brain dump" of everything that is on your mind as a to-do.
    - Write down every task that has been lingering on your mind or has an upcoming due date.
    - Keep writing until you have written down everything that's on your mind.
- For each "task," ask yourself if this is really a simple task, or is it a project?

    For example, your "task" may be "donate old clothes." Examined more closely, this task actually has several steps, so it is technically a project. These project steps may be:

- Fire up laptop.
- Open web browser.
- Perform a search for "where to donate old clothing."
- Choose a donation center from your search.
- Review the center's business hours and donation process.
- Decide on a day and time to take your donations to the center.
- Select clothes from your closet to donate.
- Take the clothes to the donation center at your designated time.
- File or notate the donation receipt with your annual income taxes.

If it's a project, write down the very next step next to the project. In this example, the next task may be to fire up your laptop.

- Is this next step something that you can do, right now?
- If not, when will you do it? Commit to taking action soon!
- Add the task to your calendar–make the appointment with yourself!
- Now keep the appointment (just like you would a dentist appointment).
- Doesn't that feel so much better?

As a Flourishing Physician, you...

- Know that motivation is not necessary for you to get something done.
- Take action regardless of your level of motivation.
- Understand the difference between a project and a task.
- Break down projects into individual tasks.
- Take action on your insights!

Chapter 5
SET AND MAINTAIN BOUNDARIES

"Never allow a person to tell you no who doesn't have the power to say yes."
–Eleanor Roosevelt

Many years ago, our family rescue dog's health began to decline quickly. He was around 13 years old at the time, so we knew the end was coming soon. If you've ever experienced an aging pet, you know how extremely difficult it is to make the decision to say goodbye. To add to the difficulty, I felt like I was making the decision alone since my divorce. I had wonderful family and friends to help, and to validate my experience, but no one else (except my daughter who was only 8 at the time) who had lived with him all the time and witnessed his day-to-day decline the way I did. Luckily, my vet was amazing and fully supported my decision to let him go. We scheduled the appointment for that Friday.

It was a Wednesday. I'll never forget taking the call from my vet while standing next to my executive assistant. She knew what was going on and what I had been struggling with over the past few weeks. As soon as I hung up the phone, I went numb. I couldn't think straight. I knew I wouldn't be able to function at work. I told her, "I need to go home right now. I'll be back at work on Monday." My executive assistant was incredible and said, "I'll make it happen. Go take care of you and your pup." I was able to spend the next few days snuggling with my dog and cherishing my last bit of time with him. It was one of the greatest gifts I ever gave myself.

I wasn't used to asking for what I needed. I wasn't used to even allowing myself to HAVE needs, let alone express them. As difficult as it was to assert myself in that moment, it was necessary for my well-being. I would have regretted not spending those last few days with my dog and allowing myself to step into how incredibly difficult that week was for me. Looking back, I also realize that I was so numb and shell-shocked by my conversation with the vet that it almost didn't matter to me how anyone else reacted to my decision to take the next few days off. I wouldn't have been able to absorb or react to anyone else's behavior or emotions at that moment.

This encounter was one of the first examples I can remember in my adult life of setting a boundary. If you're not familiar with setting boundaries for yourself, it can feel selfish and off-putting initially.

The boundaries I'm referring to are not the physical ones. One of my favorite Internet memes at the beginning of the COVID pandemic was, "When all of this is over, I still want some of you to stay 6 feet away from me." Maybe that describes you (non-huggers, rejoice!). I'm specifically referring to protecting our time, our energy, and even our emotional health.

When our boundaries are violated, we may feel hurt, betrayed, or angry…or a combination of all three. We may not even know what our boundaries are until they have been crossed.

One of my physician clients shared with me during a coaching session that she wanted to start attending a weekly Pilates class. The class was on Saturday mornings, and she told me her family expressed support for her attending. However, she was worried because she normally spent Saturday mornings catching up on charts. If she went to the class, she feared having to move her charting to a different time during the weekend, time that she would have spent with her family. She told me, "I know I am supposed to be setting a boundary, but I really can't." As she thought about setting this boundary, I asked her what feelings came up. She said she was afraid she would be perceived by her family as selfish, as failing to contribute to the family, and that she would be letting her family down. She shared with me that she thought setting a boundary was equivalent to telling her work colleagues, "That's not my job," since she saw this behavior modeled in her clinic staff. She bristled at the idea of setting boundaries at first, because she felt it went against one of her core values of teamwork.

Psychologist Dr. Becky Kennedy defines a boundary in this way: "A boundary is something you tell someone you will do, and it requires the other person to do nothing."

This is the most empowering definition and description of a boundary that I've encountered. In my example, I told my team that I would be taking the rest of the week off because of a family emergency. My boundary required them to do nothing. This was different from making a request, which may have been asking a colleague to do something in my absence. I didn't have to do that in this situation. What I love about Dr. Kennedy's definition is that it allows for us to take complete control. Because we are not asking anyone to do anything, we don't have to depend on someone else's behavior in order to set the boundary. We don't have to wait for someone to act for the boundary to be put into place. We have total control over the boundary because our behavior is the only behavior included in the equation.

Dr. Kennedy's definition can also release us from the guilt that comes up when we start to set boundaries. Physicians tend to be people who feel they need to do everything themselves. When you were in medical school, you were likely asked to perform tasks for patients that are usually carried out by someone else: starting IVs, taking vital signs, transporting patients, or running down to radiology to retrieve X-rays (if you went to medical school before digital imaging like I did!). These tasks were seen as a necessary part of our training, and we were evaluated based on our ability and willingness to say "yes" to every task asked of us (no matter how menial). We were rewarded for "being a team player" and performing these tasks that we knew were not critical components of our medical education. The thought of saying "no" to the attending or resident who asks us to carry out these tasks (that probably included fetching coffee) likely induced a great amount of fear. Chances were high that saying "no" to these tasks would have had dire consequences for our evaluation, our grades, and our future.

We've been programmed from an early age to please those around us. We were rewarded with attention and good grades for pleasing our parents and our teachers as a child. These rewards continued in our medical training; when we pleased our residents and attendings, we were more likely to receive strong recommendation letters, competitive rotations or internship programs, or highly sought-after patient cases. Our brains learn that "pleasing others" equals "getting what we want"...and we get a dopamine hit from people-pleasing.

We were hardwired to do things that someone else could have easily done. We may have even scored points on our residency application essay for a phrase such as, "I never ask someone to do something that I can do myself." These habits may have been encoded in infancy and childhood, when people-pleasing was a matter of survival. We depended on our caregivers for our every need, and if they were unhappy with us, the consequences may have been detrimental to our livelihood.

The challenge now is…we do not have enough time in the day to do all of the tasks that, yes, we can easily do. Of course you can room your own patients when your medical assistant is late or running behind. Of course you can call your patients back with normal lab values. Of course you can call the hospital to request records. I know that you are very capable and very good at doing these things! You may even enjoy those tasks on some level.

BUT…your time is limited. Performing tasks that someone else could do–and that are more aligned with their role–is not the best use of your time. Your energy is also finite, and we can quickly deplete our energy by spending time on tasks that are better suited for someone else. The frustration that comes from doing these tasks further saps our energy.

The Danger of People-Pleasing

If you always make yourself available when someone needs you, you will feel depleted rather quickly. You may have heard the phrase, "'NO' is a complete sentence." It takes energy and courage to say "no" when honoring the requests of others is not in our best interests. However, saying "no" is absolutely necessary to maintain balance in our lives. We cannot be everything to everyone and we cannot honor every request that is made of us. We may fear that the other person on the receiving end of the word "no" will be angry or will reject us. While that may be the case in the short term, in my experience, both in my own life and in the lives of my physician clients, often the other person will respect us for honoring ourselves and asserting our own needs. Over time, the more we ask for what we need, and respond in a way that meets our own interests, others will respect the new boundaries we have set. AND–even more magical–we set an example for those around us and give others permission to set their own boundaries. This can be so incredibly impactful when we are in a position of influence–parenting, leading a team, caring for patients–where we model the desired behavior and empower others along the way. If you're reading this, you are absolutely in a position of influence, whether you recognize it or not.

If you're like most people, at this point, you are starting to ask yourself how your boundaries will affect others. Our lives are so interconnected that it's next to impossible for an impactful boundary to not impact someone else…and not just anyone, usually someone that's important to us: our spouse or partner, our children, our close family or friends, our colleagues, our patients. It's important that we process these emotions (more on this in Chapter 6) and create a plan for any worries that come up.

Here's a great quote from author and researcher Daniell Koepke on this topic.

"What if they get mad at me?

If people get mad at you for having boundaries, it means they've benefitted from you not having any. You don't need to keep people happy every minute of the day. You are not responsible for other people's feelings. If someone has a reaction to your boundary, you didn't 'make' them react. You chose to voice your feelings and needs. They chose their reaction. You cannot control what other people do."

Powerful! I can't say it any better.

I can't change what another person does, but I can change how I respond. Otherwise, if I keep waiting for the other person to STOP doing what they are doing that upsets me, I'm giving away my power.

Other people's reactions reflect their own boundaries, or lack thereof. Living our lives to align with others' boundaries is a hallmark of people-pleasing behavior. Over time, a focus on pleasing others, at the expense of ourselves, leads to frustration and burnout. It is impossible to please everyone all the time!

Even if we intellectually know that we can't please everyone all the time, or even that people-pleasing is now actively getting in the way of what we want, it can be incredibly difficult to translate that knowledge into action. Our bodies have learned via the reward system that people-pleasing makes us feel good (thanks, dopamine!). The first step is to recognize and acknowledge that this thought process and this behavior are barriers to us reaching our goals. Once we acknowledge it, we can practice a different behavior (using the tools described in Chapter 3) and utilize the skills discussed in managing strong emotions (coming up in Chapter 6) to navigate through the discomfort that will arise. Working with a coach to support and encourage us can be incredibly helpful in this process.

It's key to have compassion for yourself (more on self-compassion in Chapter 6) and to honor the parts of yourself that clung to these beliefs. You may have needed those beliefs in order to literally survive or to power through a certain time period in your life. One powerful tool is to thank those parts of you that are trying to protect you. It's not only OK that this process occurs, but it's necessary, normal, and important. You cannot grow and achieve different results if your thought habits and your behaviors stay the same.

Only you will know what these thoughts and behaviors will be, and yours will probably be different from someone else's (also OK and necessary and normal). When you honor your fullest self, you create space and permission for others to do the same, which is the best gift you can give someone.

To reclaim our time and energy–resources that we don't get back once gone–it's critical that we identify, set, and maintain the boundaries that align with our well-being and our values. It takes practice and near-constant attention! As you work through this process and practice a new way of thinking, acting, and relating, please be compassionate with yourself. This work can be hard at times, but the rewards are immense.

A couple of years ago, I was coaching a physician client who was a successful, high-achieving, driven primary care physician. One of her passions was volunteering and contributing to her church congregation in different ways. During the session, she shared some frustration that she had made a commitment to a large project at church, yet she didn't want to be working on it. I asked her why she committed to it, and she said, "Because the priest asked me, and no one else wanted to do it." Her frustration centered around the fact that the project was due soon, and she said she would have to spend her entire weekend working on it, when she was behind on charts and needed to catch up…and somehow also spend time with family and get in some exercise.

I helped her explore the thoughts that led her to volunteer for this particular project. She said she felt obligated because she was asked to do it. She didn't know how to say "no." Because she felt obligated, she wasn't looking forward to it, which only increased her frustration. This project was not meaningful to her, and it was a low priority for her. It was a difficult situation all around that led her to wish she had not said "yes" when asked. She was expending a great deal of time and energy on something that didn't matter that much to her and that could have been better spent elsewhere (like with her family…her number one priority!).

She anticipated another similar ask from this priest coming up, something else that she didn't want to do. Her brain was telling her (that sneaky brain) that if she said no, the priest (with whom she had a strong friendship) wouldn't respect her and would be mad at her. I helped her question that thought. During our conversation, she had an insight that the priest, as a friend, would not want her to be feeling so frustrated and pressured. He would want her to speak up for herself and say "no" when she felt she needed to. We talked through some strategies to say "no" in a loving and kind way. The one that we crafted together was, "I'm not able to fulfill that request right now." (Say it with me: "I'm not able to fulfill that request right now.")

If you want to go for the gold, you can offer someone else who could help them. If you feel a need to justify (but you don't have to!), then you could tell the other person that you wouldn't be able to do the project justice. Again, justification is not necessary…remember that "no" is a complete sentence. Once my client established boundaries, she shared with me that she was "less guarded and more relaxed" and that she was sleeping better as a result of the reduced stress.

In one coaching session, a physician assistant client of mine shared his challenge saying "no" to leading a project that was asked of him, since he didn't have the time or resources. He came away with the phrases, "I'm honored that you came to me. I can see this is very important to you. I don't think I'm the best person for this." He felt so empowered with the idea of setting this boundary. Shortly after our conversation, he was promoted to a leadership position–a promotion which, I truly believe, would not have happened had he not established and communicated those boundaries initially.

Another physician client shared frustration that she was frequently taking work home to catch up on charts. As a primary care physician, she placed a high value on the strong relationships with her patients. She had a suspicion that if she was able to more effectively guide her conversations with patients in the exam room, she would be able to focus the interview in a way that allowed her more time to document during and after the visits. She experimented with setting a boundary and asking patients more focused questions, so that she could avoid conversations that completely derailed the visit. By setting this boundary, she didn't have to ask the patients to do anything extra, but she created additional time and space in her day, so that she could complete her charting by 5:30 p.m. and not take her laptop home in the evening.

The impact on time management here is enormous. One of my coaching clients, a successful physician leader, struggled with people-pleasing behavior and not being perceived as "difficult" by others on her team. She told me she "never says no." As a result, she was taking on work that could have easily been done by someone else–both in the clinic setting and in her leadership role. She was spending large amounts of time doing work that needed to be delegated to someone else. Once she worked through the people-pleasing tendency, she gained a significant amount of time back in her day and her week. She was able to make more progress toward her goals than she thought was possible.

Another physician client was the leader of her primary care clinic; as she set boundaries, she noted improvements in her energy. She was "not as tired and exhausted…and felt more peace and reduced stress." Even her physical health improved; her borderline-high blood pressure normalized and she experienced fewer headaches.

How does all of this relate to time management?

We waste precious time and energy on other people's agendas. If we don't set boundaries for ourselves, we can't spend our time intentionally. We relinquish power to others to dictate how we spend our time and where we put our focus. Setting and maintaining boundaries really is the keystone to all of time management; we can't manage our time effectively unless we do so.

Action Step

Grab your journal and a pen and let's get into action. You can also reference the Purposeful MD downloadable journal (https://thepurposefulmd.com/book).

- What's one boundary you can set this week? It's OK–and actually a good idea at first–to start with something small! You'll build confidence by taking small and manageable steps!
- As you think about setting this boundary, what thoughts come up? Write them all down here.
- Are these thoughts true?

- What permission do you need to give yourself to set this boundary?

As a Flourishing Physician, you...

- Recognize when you need to set a boundary.
- Release guilt that may come up when setting and maintaining a boundary.
- Realize that your time and energy are finite.
- Understand how people-pleasing may have served you in the past, but will keep you from getting what you truly want.
- Practice setting and maintaining boundaries regularly.
- Take action on your insights!

Chapter 6
MANAGE STRONG EMOTIONS

"You must do the thing you think you cannot do."
–Eleanor Roosevelt

Early in my career as a medical director, I found myself routinely in meetings or situations in which I felt my emotions run high. Often the situation was seemingly benign such as a meeting with senior leadership, where I was asked to present my monthly metrics and action plans for improvement. Sometimes, it was a much more emotionally charged situation. I clearly remember once finding out that a physician who reported to me had used a racial slur in a conversation with an applicant. I was instructed by my supervisor to inform him that this was inappropriate and that we needed to contact human resources about the incident. During my conversation with the physician, he yelled and belittled me for "making such a big deal out of nothing." I still feel my heart race just remembering the conversation. It took every ounce of strength to remain calm when my natural instinct would have been to run out of the room, find a quiet spot, curl up in a ball, and cry.

It was around this time that I began working with my executive coach. During one session, I shared my frustration that I was struggling to get a particular project off the ground. I couldn't understand why I felt stuck; I was competent in the subject matter and had all the right resources around me to succeed. My coach asked me a few questions that revealed my fear of presenting my project at a senior leadership meeting. I told her of the previous situations when I had felt attacked and belittled during these meetings. What I really wanted was a way out, some way in which I didn't have to present at, or even attend, these meetings, so I wouldn't have to feel the frustration and other strong emotions that came up for me.

Gently, she reminded me this likely wasn't possible. Attending and presenting at these meetings was part of my role and was expected of me. What would be more helpful–and would pay off in dividends throughout my career and my life–was a method to manage the strong emotions that arose during those meetings.

Managing strong emotions was a foreign concept to me at the time. I was no stranger to strong emotions–they arose all the time during my medical training–but **I had been taught to ignore them and to "power through."** There was no time to deal with strong emotions. I had to move on to the next patient, the next situation. How many times had I given bad news to a patient or family, and then immediately moved to the next room, without stopping to think or process what just happened? How many times did I run a code, console the patient's family who was watching everything, and then resume my patient rounds? I thought, that's just what we do. That's what I had seen all my clinical teachers do. We're tough, we're physicians! We can take it! We can muscle through anything. That's why we became physicians–we are built that way!

My coach was familiar with coaching physicians and was well aware that many physicians had the same mentality of "powering through." The situations physicians encounter are not situations that most people will ever face. Delivering babies and performing CPR on someone until they pass away–and everything in between–are incredibly powerful emotional experiences. She explained to me that the emotions springing from these experiences are stored in the body, and unless I acknowledge them and process them, they will have a negative impact on my ability to be creative and the best version of myself, even outside of the exam room. She also gently suggested that my "powering through" was a survival mechanism that I utilized during my training. However, when I suppress the strong negative emotions, I'm also suppressing the positive ones. I can't cherry pick to only feel the "good" feelings. True joy and happiness would only follow from allowing myself to feel and process ALL of my emotions.

Over time, with her guidance, I began to notice each time a strong emotion arose. At the coach's suggestions, I practiced acknowledging and processing those emotions in the moment. I certainly didn't hit a home run each time, but what I did notice was how much better I felt when I allowed myself to process the emotion, and how exhausted I felt when I instead ignored or suppressed ("bottled up") the emotion.

When we feel strong emotions, it's so common to try to distract ourselves...with email, social media, TV, food, shopping, or something similar. We all have these tendencies and they are natural, normal, and human. Sometimes, these distractions are a defense mechanism, because our brains and bodies can't fully take in the situation and we have to compartmentalize in the short term. Many of the physician clients I have coached admit to working in order to distract themselves from difficult emotions; one physician leader shared with me that she frequently worked long hours as an act of avoidance. Another client shared a term that she had heard for this concept–"procrasti-work" (procrastinating on important tasks by working on something else; cue the cleaning the refrigerator when I needed to study!).

Unfortunately, these distractions will make us feel better temporarily, but in the long term, those emotions don't go away. They are stored in our bodies. Emotions are like a beach ball that you try to hold underwater. The longer you hold it under water, the more energy it takes, and the more likely it is to pop up and hit you in the face. Emotions are the same way; they stay with us and we expend a lot of energy to push them down. Once they surface, they pack more punch than they would have initially.

Negative emotions can evoke the fight-or-flight response from our nervous system. This is an evolutionary response to a threat–real or perceived–which sets off a cascade of hormones coursing through our bodies. These hormones allow us to escape the threat–such as a bear chasing us–but these hormones also shut off our ability to be creative and think clearly.

The challenge is, with ongoing stress, our bodies remain in fight-or-flight mode, leading to increased anxiety, fatigue, and burnout. Many times, we don't have control over the stressors. However, we can–and must–counteract the negative effect of the stress hormones.

It's unrealistic to expect to never feel these emotions. They are a part of life. We can't know what it means to feel happy unless we know how it feels to be unhappy.

What we can do is manage our response to them–how we allow them to work through our body. This will allow us to not get stuck in negative emotions but to work through them so we can act more appropriately.

There are some well-researched ways to do this, excellently described by Drs. Emily and Amelia Nagoski in a book called *Burnout: The Secret to Unlocking the Stress Cycle*. They describe "completing the stress cycle" to process strong emotions that are stored in the body. They suggest any of the following: any physical movement, sleep, deep breathing for 1-2 minutes (ideally where the exhale is longer than the inhale), crying (it's a great release of emotions), laughing/watching a funny video or show, or some type of actual connection to another being (snuggling with a pet, hugging a loved one, etc.). Since strong emotions activate our fight-or-flight response, the above activities will soothe the sympathetic nervous system and activate our parasympathetic response, signaling to our bodies that the threat is over and that we are physically safe.

These are wonderful tools that I've utilized throughout my life (I've already mentioned how much of an outlet running is for me) and have encouraged my clients, and patients, to employ as well. While these tools are incredibly helpful and useful, their utility "in the moment" is limited. When I'm confronted with a colleague yelling in my face during a meeting, it's not realistic that I will be able to go for a run or go home to snuggle with my dog (oh, how I wish!). What we also need are tools to deal with the strong emotion in the moment so that we can still think clearly and respond appropriately. Then, when the threat is removed, we can allow ourselves to process and complete the stress cycle.

The first step is to breathe. This sounds simple, but so often in fight-or-flight mode, we are actually holding our breath. You will calm your sympathetic and activate your parasympathetic nervous system if the exhale is longer than the inhale. Inhaling for a count of 1 and exhaling for a count of 2 is a perfect "hack" in the moment to signal to the body that you are safe.

The next step is to name the emotion. It doesn't have to be complicated. "Anger" or "fear" or even "strong" are perfect labels. You can always go back later and identify the emotion more clearly, if that's helpful.

The third step is to acknowledge the difficulty. Find whatever works for you. My favorite is "This is really hard." Others may say something like, "It's hard to be human," or "You're not alone."

The fourth–optional, but very helpful–step is to self-soothe. A great way to do this (especially helpful for situations where you don't want to draw attention to yourself) is to gently touch one hand with the other. It's another wonderful way to signal to the body that you are safe and that you are being cared for.

The last step is to choose your next action. How would you like to respond? For the colleague yelling at you, it may be, "It's not OK for you to speak to me that way," or "I will not be yelled at."

Completing all these steps can take only a few seconds but can drastically change your body chemistry and subsequently your response to a threat (real or perceived–to the brain it doesn't matter).

At the beginning of a recent coaching session with a physician client, I asked her what she would like to accomplish during our call. She said, "I don't want to get angry when my colleague doesn't do what I ask her to do." I hear this a lot from my clients, telling me they don't want to have a certain emotion (usually anger, fear, or frustration). It's understandable; these emotions are uncomfortable, and we tend to move away from discomfort.

One of my roles as her coach was to share the truth with her, even when that truth may not be what she wants to hear. The truth I shared with her was that I was unable to prevent her from getting angry. She was unable to prevent herself from getting angry. Anger is a normal human emotion that we will all encounter at some point in our lives. Understandably, difficult emotions are just that–difficult. They are uncomfortable. We don't like to feel them. When we do, it's natural to want to make them go away. To exacerbate this discomfort, my client had been socialized that, as a woman, she's not permitted to show her anger. She didn't feel safe expressing her anger and, as a result, the anger was building up in her body and expressing itself in other ways.

Her real challenge wasn't the anger itself; it was how she acted when she let the anger take control of her. It was also what she was telling herself about the anger. She was telling herself, "I shouldn't be angry. What my colleague was doing wasn't that bad. No one else around me is angry. It's wrong to be angry." Those thoughts about her anger, layered on top of the anger itself, were compounding her frustration and adding to the difficulty.

The first step was giving herself permission to feel anger. I reminded her that her feelings are all normal and allowed. Her thought of "I shouldn't be angry" was increasing her frustration and piling on top of the discomfort.

I guided her through the steps I described above that she can use as often as needed to process the strong emotions that she was feeling. We used the tools during our session to work with the emotions that were arising as she was describing her situation. She immediately noted that she felt so much more peaceful and grounded, even though nothing had changed about the actual situation. She was able to think clearly through her next steps and was more confident to move forward and handle the situation in a way that aligned with her values. She came back to our next session having practiced the steps and told me how much lighter, happier, peaceful, and less stressed she felt overall.

Another physician client who was in a leadership position shared some strong emotions that were coming up as she was having ongoing conversations with a physician in her clinic that was not meeting expectations and required intervention. She relayed to me that, during one tense conversation, she felt herself become triggered, and she was able to notice this in the form of tension in her neck. Once she noticed this tension, she grounded herself by taking slow, deep breaths. This simple grounding exercise allowed her to respond more thoughtfully and handle the situation in a way that was more aligned with her values. She realized how many of her emotions she had been suppressing all along, and she now understands that strong emotions are not inherently bad–they are simply signals. In her case, the emotion was a signal that she needed a slow, deep breath in that moment. Once she allowed herself this slow breath, she was able to respond much more intentionally.

Prioritizing the time and space to process strong emotions is critical to our overall health. The negative impact of chronic stress on physical and emotional health is well-researched. What's also evident from research is that we can't selectively suppress emotions. When we suppress negative ones, we suppress positive ones too. We can't allow ourselves to feel the good ones unless we also allow ourselves to feel the tough ones.

Working with strong emotions requires daily practice and attention. Just like anything new, initially it will likely feel uncomfortable. With continued practice, it gets easier and becomes more automatic.

Self-Compassion

As you practice, it is imperative that you are kind and loving with yourself. The tool of self-compassion is critical as you practice and take action on all of the concepts described in this book. Dr. Kristin Neff, self-compassion expert and researcher, defines self-compassion as "simply the process of turning compassion inward." We treat ourselves the way we would treat a good friend.

How often are we compassionate toward ourselves? Do we treat ourselves as kindly as we treat others? Many of us have a critical internal voice that judges our actions, thoughts, and emotions. We justify it by telling ourselves that this critical voice keeps us from making mistakes and ensures we maintain high standards for ourselves. We utilize what journalist and meditation champion Dan Harris calls our "internal cattle prod" that, in our minds, has allowed us to be successful by pushing us harder and harder and raising the expectations higher and higher. The truth is, this "internal cattle prod" may work to a point but it's not the voice that will sustain us in the long term. This voice leads to shame which will eventually lead us to shut down and stop taking action that will help us reach our goals.

Spoiler alert…we are human and we will make mistakes! When we inevitably do, how often do we speak to ourselves in a kind voice? Or are we more likely to speak to ourselves in a critical or harsh tone?

A great question to ask ourselves is: if a loved one came to us, having made the same mistake, would we speak critically and harshly to her? Or would we be kind and compassionate toward her?

We devalue ourselves when we are critical and judgmental of our own behavior. Self-compassion, on the other hand, is empowering and allows us to be kinder to others, less stressed, and more productive. Self-compassion is a skill that can be learned and developed with practice. Similarly to managing our strong emotions, the more we practice, the easier self-compassion becomes, and the more likely we are to hold ourselves with compassion even when it is difficult.

How does all of this relate to time management?

In order for us to be intentional and purposeful about how we spend our time, we have to process the strong emotions that arise. When we numb the emotions, we move away from our values and away from what lights us up. We can't make intentional choices about where to focus if we are suppressing strong emotions and judging ourselves for doing so.

Action Step

Let's get into action. You can also reference the Purposeful MD downloadable journal (https://thepurposefulmd.com/book).

Visualize a recent situation in which you noticed a strong emotion arise, and practice these steps.

- Take a deep breath. Breathe so that your exhale is longer than your inhale (inhale for a count of 1/exhale for a count of 2; or inhale for a count of 2/exhale for a count of 4).
- Name the emotion. Keep it simple for now.
- Acknowledge that this is hard, with a simple phrase like "this is really hard," or "it's tough to be human," or "you're not alone."
- Soothe yourself in whatever way is helpful (and possible

in the moment). Practice different techniques: such as gently rubbing one hand with the other, stroking your arm, or giving yourself a big hug.
- Choose your next action with a clear mind.

As a Flourishing Physician, you:
- Recognize that all emotions are part of being human.
- Know that you can't suppress negative emotions without suppressing positive ones.
- Are gentle with yourself when strong emotions arise.
- Practice processing strong emotions in the moment when they arise.
- Engage in activities to allow stress to move through your body.
- Take action on your insights!

Chapter 7
CREATE YOUR OWN CONFIDENCE

"Be confident, not certain."
–Eleanor Roosevelt

My first exposure to the notion of confidence was as a small girl, watching what became one of my favorite movies, *The Sound of Music*. Near the beginning, the young nun Maria was assigned as a governess to the wealthy von Trapp family. Having no experience as a governess, Maria tried to decline the order, to no avail. Knowing that she didn't have a choice in the matter (for the time being, anyway!), she decided to take the challenge head-on. She sings a powerful "pump-me-up" song called "I Have Confidence" as she dances to the von Trapp family estate. We all know how the movie ends: she endears herself to the children and to the Captain and joins the family.

What I love about this scene, but didn't fully appreciate

until I was an adult, was that Maria CREATED her own confidence. She didn't wait for confidence to fall out of the sky. She created confidence in various ways through the span of the song. She validated her fears, talked to herself using empowering language, and engaged in physical activity (walking/dancing) to boost dopamine and adrenaline.

Confidence is similar to motivation in this way. We tell ourselves, "I don't have the confidence," or "I wish I had the confidence," as if this feeling just magically appears. We know that doesn't happen, and if we wait for it, we will miss out on so many opportunities and joys in our lives.

So, how do we build confidence?

The most effective way to build confidence is to act.

I'll say it again for the people in the back:

The most effective way to build confidence is to act.

What kind of action is necessary? Most of the time, the actions that build confidence are those that also lead to some level of fear. As we discussed in the last chapter, setting and maintaining a boundary can be scary at first. Saying "no" to taking that extra shift. Leaving work 15 minutes early to attend your child's soccer game. Closing your door so you can actually eat lunch without interruptions. Asking your supervisor for a raise or extra administrative time to cover the medical director role you took last year. All of these actions build confidence over time.

Here's the truth: actions precede confidence. One falsehood

we tell ourselves that it's the other way around–we have to be confident first before we can act. Listen to any podcast or interview with someone who took a risk that paid off–Bill Gates, Oprah Winfrey, Barack Obama–and you will hear a common theme. They all acted BEFORE they developed full confidence. Their confidence was a RESULT of the action that they took.

Remember your first year of medical school, walking into the standardized patient room to take your first history? I still get butterflies in my stomach when I picture that door and I can still remember how terrified I was. Now I can take patient histories without even thinking about what to say next–it's so automatic. That's because I've done the same actions over and over and the pathways are wired into my brain.

Taking action helps us move out of our comfort zone. We tend to, unknowingly, create our own obstacles when we stay in our comfort zone. I know my comfort zone is such a great place to be! That's why it's called "the comfort zone!" Who doesn't love to live in comfort? I know I do! Staying in the zone of our expertise is alluringly comfortable, and it becomes harder to venture out, but stepping outside our comfort zone is actually what we need in order to get what we want.

The truth is we don't grow when we stay in our comfort zone. Humans are meant to grow and learn and flourish. We used to think that adults didn't have much capacity for learning, but we now know the opposite is true. We are wired this way. It's when we think we "know everything" that we stop learning. I love the quote by Zen master Shunryu Suzuki, "In the beginner's mind there are many possibilities, but in the expert's, there are few." When we approach a problem with a beginner's mind, we are open to any and all possibilities; we have access to creative parts of our brain that we wouldn't otherwise have access to. There's a concept called confirmation bias, which says that once we have our mind made up about something, we close ourselves off to other ideas. This can have devastating consequences in the field of medicine if we fail to diagnose correctly because our minds are closed off to any new information.

Why does this matter? We can't be our best selves from our comfort zone. We are meant to do so many wonderful and creative and inspiring things. Think of any innovation that makes our lives easier and improves the world around us. Those innovations didn't come about by someone staying small and safe. They were borne out of risk-taking and the quest for more knowledge and learning.

Break out of your comfort zone. Think of one thing that is slightly scary and slightly exciting, and go for it. It can be something small, like asking a colleague that you'd like to get to know better to join you for coffee before work, or something big, like leaving your comfortable employed position to start your own practice where you call the shots. If you are a member of the human race, you will notice thoughts that are telling you things like, "I can't do this. It's too scary. People won't like me. No one will care." Think of these thoughts as gremlins who are doing their job to keep your nervous system safe. Those thoughts served you at one point in your life and helped you survive when you were younger.

BUT: you don't need to hear from them. You are higher on the evolutionary scale! Look those gremlins in the eyes, thank them for trying to keep you safe and tell them, "Thanks gremlins. I've got this. I know what I'm doing."

As you begin to take action, despite not feeling confident (yet), you are developing your belief in yourself. You are teaching yourself that you can trust yourself to both take necessary action and keep yourself safe. Your self-confidence will blossom and flourish as a result.

One of my clients, a nurse practitioner leader, was asked to present at a large forum of other nurse practitioners and physician assistants. After her presentation, she shared with me that she had initially been nervous, but then remembered that one of her strengths is public speaking. In the act of remembering, her anxiety lessened. After the presentation, her confidence blossomed. The act of doing the thing that made her nervous actually made her more confident. She became confident AFTER acting, not before.

How does all of this relate to time management?

When we rely on an outside influence or wait for confidence to "strike" before taking action, we wait too long. We are relinquishing our power to an outside force instead of taking back the power that we hold in our hands. We can't make intentional choices about how to spend our time and energy when we relinquish this power.

Action Step

Grab your journal and a pen and let's get into action. You can also reference the Purposeful MD downloadable journal (https://thepurposefulmd.com/book).

- What's one thing that feels slightly scary, that you've been putting off or you know is important for you to do? (Practice with something only slightly scary. As you build confidence, you can up the fear factor.)
- Picture yourself taking this action. Make your vision as vivid as possible. What will you be wearing? What will the weather be like? Who else will be there?
- Write down when you will do this and add it to your calendar.
- Immediately before, schedule one activity that will give you a physical boost (dancing, singing, movement).
- Journal afterwards. What came up for you? Did you notice the gremlins? What did you tell them? How do you feel?

Keep taking action. As you do, your confidence grows naturally, and your impact on yourself, your close circle, and the world expands immensely. That's what this world needs– more women physicians owning their power, their worth, and taking action for the good of others.

As a Flourishing Physician, you:

- Recognize that we create our own confidence.
- Know that taking action is the only true way to build and sustain confidence.
- Break out of your comfort zone to experience growth.
- Take action on your insights!

Chapter 8
GET THE REST YOU NEED

"It isn't enough to talk about peace. One must believe in it. And it isn't enough to believe in it. One must work at it."
–Eleanor Roosevelt

As I mentioned previously, I injured my knee in late 2020 and had to pause running. Because running is such an outlet for me, I knew I had to pursue treatment so I could get back on the pavement.

A visit with an orthopedic surgeon in January 2021 offered a few options–him being a surgeon, naturally, one of the options was surgery. I clearly remember the feeling of sitting on the examination table, and him being incredibly patient with me as I weighed the options. I thought to myself, "Well, at least if I have surgery, I'll get a few days off to rest. A couple days in the hospital sounds kind of nice."

NICE?? In the middle of a surge of the worst infectious pandemic in the past 100 years, I thought a hospital stay sounded "NICE"? (Granted, I had recently received my second COVID vaccine and was feeling rather invincible.)

I look back and realize that's how exhausted I was. My body so desperately needed relief that I felt I needed to have surgery and stay in a hospital for a few days to give myself permission to rest. It was as if I could rest only if I had a *really* valid reason, and only if I finished my chores first!

I wish I could say that moment was a turning point for me, and that I prioritized rest from that day on. Instead, this story turned out to have a much more impactful message that I can only appreciate in hindsight. I continued to work myself beyond exhaustion in the months after that orthopedic visit. I was participating in a fundraising campaign for a charity near and dear to my heart, planning a wedding, studying to become a certified coach, reeling from the pandemic (like much of the world), *and* I was grieving the recent passing of my father. Only now as I write those words does the gravity and overwhelm of that time really sink in. This constant "go-go-go" did later manifest as mental and physical health challenges...in other words, my body catching up to the trauma and stress.

I thought that my lack of rest was a sign of success. I thought, "I've got so much on my plate. I can't stop now. I have to keep the momentum going. I have to sign up for an elective surgical procedure to allow myself a few days off."

I was mistaking my productivity for my self-worth... defining myself in terms of what I can accomplish.

I now realize that my worth is not defined by my productivity.

I'll repeat it because it's that important.

My worth is not defined by my productivity. I am worthy of rest, no matter what.

Your worth is not defined by your productivity. You are worthy of rest, no matter what.

American "hustle" culture is so ingrained with the notion that productivity and accomplishments are real measures of our worth and value in society. Have you ever spent time in another culture that values rest as much as work? Many European countries highly cherish rest and build it into their day (the afternoon siesta as an example). The United States continues to be the only developed country that does not guarantee paid vacation.

The medical culture amplifies this outdated mentality. When I was training, it was not uncommon to regularly work a 36-hour shift–working all day and all night and all day the following day. We were expected to be awake and available at all times during the shift. The lack of rest was not only expected but celebrated and glorified. It was the kiss of death on a medical rotation to fall asleep during morning rounds or afternoon lectures after being awake for 24 hours or more. Outside of this, we were regularly expected to deny our bodily needs to attend to the needs of patients or our colleagues, skipping meals to see patients or scrub into cases. And no way would we ask for a break in a long surgical case to use the restroom. Asking to attend to our physical needs was unheard of.

This mentality and practice can't be good for patient care either. How many of you would want a physician who has been awake for 36 hours to take care of you or your family member? We now know that being awake for that long has the same effect on the brain and our reaction time as being legally drunk. Unfortunately, there are incidents of patient harm occurring in these scenarios, which are both heartbreaking and completely preventable.

Our bodies and our brains need rest. For us to be at our best selves, we must rest. Rest will look different for different people. For me, rest can mean sleeping, meditating, journaling, reading a good book, taking a hot bath, spending time in nature, getting a massage, practicing gentle yoga, or stretching. The amount and type of rest we need at different points in our lives will change. I had major surgery in the summer of 2022, and for many weeks after my procedure, I was amazed at how much sleep I seemed to need every night. My body was healing, and it was important that I honor my needs, even if it meant going to sleep at 8 p.m. every night for a few months.

Do you ever wonder why babies and small children need so much sleep? Their brains are taking in so much new information that they tire out very quickly. When we are in a phase of personal and professional growth–stretching our brains–we may find that we need more rest than at other times, and this is perfectly normal.

One of my physician coaching clients was struggling in almost every aspect of her life. She was a busy full-time clinician who was frustrated that she consistently had unaddressed patient messages and incomplete charts. She was a wife and mother who lamented that she didn't have enough time to spend with her family in the evenings and on weekends, because she was frequently catching up on work. Because of her stress, she wasn't enjoying her patient interactions any longer, despite loving her relationships with her patients. She found herself getting easily frustrated and snapping at people around her. What she wanted from me was some help in managing her stress.

One of my first questions to her was about her sleep. She told me that she was staying awake until 12 or 1 a.m. working on charts and then waking up at 5 a.m. to "get ahead" of the day's schedule. On weekends, she allowed herself a bit more sleep, but not much; she would wake up at 6 a.m. instead of 5.

In a loving way, I let her know that the absolute first step to managing her stress was to allow herself the sleep she needs. As a physician, she knew intellectually that she wasn't sleeping enough, but she justified it by telling herself (and me) that she needed that time to catch up on work. I reminded her of how important her sleep was, and that nothing in her life would work smoothly unless she slept as much as she needed.

She resisted at first, but eventually agreed with me. I asked her what the first step would be to ensuring she got the sleep she needed. We spent the entire hour-long session creating a plan so that she would be in bed by 10 p.m., ready for sleep (not in bed watching TV or scrolling on her phone). Only if she was fully rested would she even begin to be able to tackle the other areas of stress in her life. During our next session, she shared that she implemented the strategies and was sleeping much better than she had previously, feeling more productive and less stressed throughout the day.

Another physician client described looking forward to an upcoming weekend off, where her family would be out of town and she would have the house to herself. She described herself as an "active relaxer"–that she preferred staying busy to recharge. We discussed that her desired form of rest may not always be sleep, and she did note that she tended to not rest until "everything is in order." She was concerned that she would be too "overwhelmed" by the disorganization in her house to be able to relax and recharge. By the end of our session, she committed to hiring someone to clean the house so she could better utilize the time for herself. She told me that "rest is medicine" and "it's OK to take care of myself."

Often, under stress and when life gets busy, sleep is one of the first areas that we sacrifice. We think we can operate with a sleep deficit, but as medical professionals, we know that this isn't the case. We cannot function unless we are sleeping well. There may be periods (new parents, I'm talking to you!) when we just can't get the sleep we need, but this must be temporary. We must prioritize sleep for optimal physical, emotional, and mental health. Lack of sleep will further compound the stress in our bodies. I've experienced personally that every aspect of my life is just better and easier when I'm sleeping and resting to the extent that my body needs.

How does all of this relate to time management?

We are HUMAN and WE NEED REST.

We are HUMAN and WE NEED REST.

We are HUMAN and WE NEED REST.

Read that sentence over and over again, as many times as you need, so that you can feel it in your bones.

Action Step

Grab your journal and a pen and let's get into action. You can also reference the Purposeful MD downloadable journal (https://thepurposefulmd.com/book).

- Write down how many hours of sleep, on average, you have gotten over the past 14 days. If needed, track your sleep for 14 days and come back to this exercise.
- If your lifestyle allows, allow yourself to wake naturally, without an alarm (electronic, human, or furry) for the next 14 days, and notice how many hours of sleep you got on those nights. That's the amount of sleep you need most nights to feel your best self. Most people need 7-9 hours of sleep per night for optimal health.

- If you are regularly getting less sleep than you need, commit to optimizing your sleep.
- Identify ways you can create more restorative sleep. Shut off screens 1 hour before bedtime, don't stay in bed unless you are asleep or engaged in intimate activities with your partner, and cut back on caffeine and alcohol.
- Try meditation or journaling before bed to put your mind in a more relaxed state.
- Talk to your family about the importance of sleep and involve them if you need any changes to routines (mealtimes, curfew, TV, etc.).
- Keep practicing until you are feeling more rested.
- Talk with your primary care provider if you notice continued difficulties sleeping.

As a Flourishing Physician, you:

- Understand how important sleep is to your overall functioning.
- Prioritize sleep over almost any other activity.
- Practice daily habits to get the sleep you need.
- Take action on your insights!

Further Reading

https://cepr.net/report/no-vacation-nation-revised/

Chapter 9
DEVELOP MORE FOUNDATIONAL HABITS

"Do what you feel in your heart to be right–for you'll be criticized anyway."
–Eleanor Roosevelt

I've noticed an interesting pattern that has emerged over the past several years. Life just always seems to be smoother when I'm consistent with a few key habits. These would be what I call my foundational habits, my non-negotiables. They are necessary for me to function at my best and are habits in which I participate every day. My foundational habits are daily meditation, at least 5 glasses of water daily, and regular exercise (at least 3 times a week for 30 minutes in each session).

I've gone through periods where I am more consistent with these habits, alternating with periods where I'm less consistent. What's interesting to notice is that, unsurprisingly,

I'm able to manage my emotions and stress levels SO MUCH more easily when I engage with these habits regularly. The other interesting notion that I've realized is that I have a tendency to get off track when things are "going well" in life. Inevitably, then some stressor pops up, and I'm more reactive to it since I've been inconsistent with my habits. Then, because "things are crazy," I'm less inclined to restart the foundational habits, setting up a vicious cycle where my stress increases and I'm less equipped to manage it effectively.

With the support of coaches, therapists, and loved ones, I'm now more able to quickly get "back on track" in a non-judgmental way. Life happens. We can't always control what life throws at us. What we can control–and the **only** thing we can control–is how we respond. The more consistent I am with my foundational habits, no matter what is swirling around me at the moment, the more grounded and stable I am, and the better I am able to manage life's curveballs.

Those curveballs will keep coming! I'm able to handle them more effectively because of how I respond. Through years of coaching and working on managing my stress and emotions, I've learned, not just intellectually but also experientially, how important it is to prioritize my own emotional and physical health. Carving out time for myself is not at all selfish. It is absolutely necessary in order to keep all the metaphorical plates spinning in my life. I can't continue to serve others–as a physician, coach, mom, wife, and other roles–unless I'm caring for myself first and foremost.

In addition to my foundational habits, I have several other habits that I consider extra tools in my toolbelt that help me manage stress when it arises. Note that these are in addition to the non-negotiable, foundational habits; these are "use as needed, early and often."

I keep a list on my phone that I can pull out when I feel stressed. I've practiced each of these enough to know that they help me feel grounded so I can respond in an authentic way to whatever life is throwing at me. Similar to the list that Drs. Emily and Amelia Nagoski shared on completing the stress cycle, there is scientific evidence to show that these actions create safety in the body.

Plus, there's evidence within ME (n=1) that they make me feel better!

Here's my list–note that it's specific enough that I don't have to make any decisions (e.g., how long should I meditate?) once I've chosen an action.

- Take a 10-minute walk.
- Spend 10 minutes outside in the sun (easy to do year-round when you live in Texas like me!).
- Meditate for 5 minutes.
- Journal for 5 minutes.
- Take a 20-minute power nap.
- Snuggle with my dog.
- Do 2 Sun salutations.

- Listen to my Amazon playlist of songs that make me feel happy.
- Text a close friend to say hello.

What would you include on your list? We will do some journaling on this at the end of the chapter.

Play–Just for the Fun of it

I remember once, about 10 years ago, someone asked me what my hobbies were, and I was stumped. I had no idea. I was a relatively new attending physician, medical director, and single mom to a young daughter. Hobbies? Who has time for those? I'll get to those someday…when I finish all my work!

Interestingly, it was the dating scene after my divorce that first spurred me to consider what my hobbies were. In order to appear interesting on my dating profiles, I felt I had to come up with something as a hobby other than "reading a Brené Brown book and then journaling while I cry my eyes out because SHE GETS ME."

Can you relate?

When you hear the word "play," what images come to mind for you? Is it children running around a playground on a sunny day? Is it a baseball game or tennis match? Is it implied that play is only for children? What about professional athletes? Would they consider their sport "play" even though it's literally their job?

Up until a few years ago, my image of play involved some

outcome or score, or it even required some type of justification. We put our kids in sports so that they can learn discipline and teamwork. Another person plays so that she can earn a paycheck or a spot on the team. I didn't see play as something I could do merely for its own sake. It seemed childish, maybe even immature. I'm too busy for that! Or so I thought.

There's a beautiful concept called "flow" described in the book *Flow* by Mihaly Csikszentmihalyi. He describes "flow" as "a state in which people are so involved in an activity that nothing else seems to matter; the experience is so enjoyable that people will continue to do it even at great cost, for the sheer sake of doing it." In the state of flow, time loses all sense of meaning. We can literally get lost in the act of play.

The truth was, at the time of my dating profile creation, I had hobbies, and I was playing, but I didn't see it that way. Running had become a big part of my life. I loved the physical outlet and the community of people I had met. I loved challenging myself and regularly training for races (I ran typically one half-marathon per year). I just didn't see running as PLAY. In my mind, it was also a means to an end: a way to stay in shape, to relieve stress, and to meet interesting people.

When I first discovered doing an activity merely for the sake of doing it, it seemed like a crazy concept. For a high-achieving, driven person like me, it just didn't compute. I felt that everything I did had to have a reason, a purpose. The reason couldn't simply be, "because I like doing this." That felt selfish, self-absorbed.

I was too busy to PLAY; I was building my career, getting my MBA, raising my daughter, attempting to date, maintaining a 60-year-old house, prioritizing my own physical and emotional health, and spending time with family and friends.

I started to view running differently. I began to pay more attention to the flow state I would achieve, sometimes referred to as the "runner's high." I celebrated myself for prioritizing running and acknowledged the "great cost" of time, energy, happy hours, and crazy looks from non-runners who didn't understand why I would skip Friday happy hour and wake up at 5 a.m. on a Saturday to run 10 miles when I wasn't being chased.

And you know what? I enjoyed running more. I viewed it as more of a choice and less of a burden. I reminded myself, "I'm doing this because I want to." I expressed my gratitude to the universe for providing me with the ability and the means to run, not to mention the amazing fellow runners I have met over the years.

When you think of a flow state, what comes up for you? Another way to ask the question is–what did you enjoy doing as a child? Painting? Playing or creating music? Reading? Gardening? Hiking? Playing a sport? Children are often lost in flow when doing something they enjoy–and they may not even realize it. I remember often hearing the phrase "time flies when you're having fun" during my childhood…a less refined description of flow. Take some time to think of something you once loved doing and, if you've stopped doing that activity, think how you could incorporate it back into your life. If you haven't played ANYTHING since hopscotch in preschool, it's definitely time to build play back into your life.

Play is not just for kids; it's important for adults' brains too. It's really unfortunate that play for adults is often seen as self-serving and unnecessary. Play helps us become more creative and allows us to regulate our emotions more effectively. It can relieve stress and even strengthen our relationships. Besides that, it's just plain fun!

As you are thinking about what these habits could mean for you, notice the thoughts that come up for you. Maybe you are telling yourself:

I don't have time.
It's selfish to spend time on myself.
I'm not good at it anymore.
It costs too much money.
People will think I'm crazy.
I don't have access to (equipment, materials, tools).

Remember we talked about thoughts in Chapter 3…these thoughts are automatic, generated by your brain to keep you safe. These thoughts probably make you feel defeated, insecure, or anxious. Those feelings aren't great starting points!

Instead, you can choose a new thought that will empower you to take action toward your goals, a thought that makes you feel confident and hopeful.

What's a new thought you can choose?

I need to care for myself so that I can care for others.

I can carve out 5 minutes per day for myself.

These habits will serve me and serve everyone around me.

I haven't done (activity) in a while, but it doesn't matter, it will be fun.

Maybe others will join me!

I can borrow (equipment, materials) from someone to get started.

I was coaching a physician client who had recently received a promotion; as she settled into her new role and her new schedule, she expressed frustration that she had stopped exercising and was feeling physically sluggish as a result. She was a runner and had previously run 5Ks and 10Ks and really missed running and training for races. I noticed how excited she was when talking about running. It was clear this was something she wanted to resume. I asked her what was holding her back from something she wanted to do. She replied, "I don't know when and where I would run. I'm afraid I'd be really slow at first. I need to find time to find a race and a training plan and sign up for it."

Her brain had created these thoughts and stopped her from moving forward before she even started. She had already talked herself out of running!

Even as she was speaking the thoughts out loud, she was able to examine and question them. She decided these thoughts were not serving her, and she created new thoughts. "It doesn't matter if I'm slow; what's important is that I'm doing it. I'll run three times a week: twice during the week in the morning, and once on a weekend morning. There's a path near my house that I'd love to try," she said.

The best part of our session was her getting into action. While we were on the call, she looked up a local race that was a couple of months away and happened to be the day after her birthday (something to celebrate!). She signed up for the race and downloaded the free training plan that came along with it. She then added the runs to her calendar and committed to herself that she would follow through. She asked if she could check in with me to stay accountable and I wholeheartedly said "yes." Accountability is one of the magic ingredients of coaching!

How does all of this relate to time management?

Our foundational habits prime our brains and our bodies so that we make choices that align with our highest selves. We will be more purposeful with our time and energy and spend it in ways that intentionally create joy. When we engage in play, we access creative parts of our brains that we don't often tap into. These parts of our brains allow us to make new connections and think in different ways.

Action Step

Grab your journal and a pen and let's get into action. You can also reference the Purposeful MD downloadable journal (https://thepurposefulmd.com/book).

- What are your foundational habits that keep you grounded? Nourishing food, adequate sleep, regular physical activity, meditation, hydration, and carving out

time for play are great examples.
- Is there any one of those habits that has gotten off track for you recently? Or that you'd like to start? Pick the one that most resonates with you.
- What are 1-2 foundational habits that are non-negotiable for you and that you will commit to regularly?
- What needs to happen for you to stay accountable? (Checking in with someone, adding the actions to your calendar or task list, etc.)
- Commit to yourself that you will do this!
- Bonus journaling!
  - Create a list of 5-7 specific actions you can take when you are stressed. These actions MUST be actions you can take in the middle of a busy workday. Even "take 3 deep breaths" is a great start.
  - Keep this digital or paper list with you at all times.
  - Practice the next time you feel stress in the body and notice how it feels.

As a Flourishing Physician, you:
- Know how important foundational habits are for overall well-being.
- Create a plan and stick to it!
- Recognize that play isn't just for kids.
- Take specific actions in the moment to reduce stress in the body.
- Take action on your insights!

Chapter 10
LET GO OF WHAT'S NOT WORKING

"No one can make you feel inferior without your consent."
–Eleanor Roosevelt

I live in South Texas, and this past winter, we experienced a deep freeze. Our semi-tropical plants are not used to this extreme cold, and many trees and plants in yards around the city don't survive freezing temperatures. Once the weather begins to warm (which is usually as early as February), my husband and I will take on the task of cleaning up the yard (either ourselves or with hired help). We prune dead branches, remove dead shrubs and small trees, pull weeds that somehow managed to survive, and rake or blow away fallen leaves. It's quite a project, which I equally dread and enjoy. The dread comes from the frustration that these plants, which created lovely blooms for much of the year, are being chopped to the roots. The enjoyment comes from the fact that immediately after the work is complete, our yard looks emptier but somehow more inviting and beautiful. It's like we've made room for the new branches and buds to arrive. We've removed what's not growing so that we can make space for what is. It's such a metaphor for life. So much of the time, the best course of action is not to add, but to subtract.

When we feel frustrated, overwhelmed, or anxious, we often try to squash those emotions by doing something. We act so that we don't notice the difficult emotions. The actions can vary from person-to-person: eating, drinking, shopping, scrolling social media, bingeing Netflix, overworking. Regardless of the action, the end result is usually adding some level of stimulation to our lives. How often does that work to reduce the emotions? In the short term, maybe sometimes–we may temporarily suppress the emotion or distract ourselves– but in the long term, almost never.

What if we just stop, instead of increasing the stimulation by doing something? What if we attempt to subtract, rather than add? What if we invite some quiet into our day? What if we notice the stimulants that may be increasing our level of anxiety, including our own thoughts and people around us? What if we gave ourselves permission to *let go*?

Just as we cleared away the dead branches and leaves in our yard, to allow the new blooms to come in, we have to clear away the "dead space" and clutter in our minds, and in our lives, to make room for the new. We have to let go of what's not serving us, so that we, in turn, can bloom.

Knowing what to clear away–what to let go of–is one of the most powerful aspects of personal growth and development. There's a beautiful quote from the *Tao Te Ching*:

"The world belongs to those who let go." For us to invite the new into our lives, we have to let go of thoughts, attitudes, beliefs, behaviors, and even people that are no longer serving us. They may be actively holding us back from becoming the person we truly want to become. What makes this so difficult is that often these thoughts, attitudes, etc. did serve us at some point in our lives. They may have helped us to get where we currently are. Because of this, we may feel a tremendous amount of guilt when beginning to let go. We may feel that we have to hold onto these things in order to reach our goals. By letting go, we may fear we are hurting others in our lives, and fear the loss or repercussions.

As we've already discussed in the book, we must acknowledge the fear and notice that our egos are trying to keep us safe. Remember, this strategy worked for us at some point in our lives, but it's no longer working. We are growing and changing, and what we are growing toward and moving toward does not fit the mold that fit us once before. We are like a nautilus that grows and no longer fits the shell that kept it safe and protected. As we grow, we have to break free from the shell, let that shell go, and allow ourselves to become the people we were meant to be.

I was recently traveling home from a retreat. While packing, I became frustrated when my belongings seemingly wouldn't fit in my suitcase. I had a few more objects on the return trip (hello, retreat swag!), but not enough that my suitcase shouldn't close. Struggling with the zipper on the suitcase, I realized what a metaphor this is for our time and energy. I know that if my stuff won't fit in the suitcase, I have to remove some items. I can't take everything that I want with me, or I'll need a bigger suitcase (not an option on the return trip!).

Similarly, **our time and energy are finite**. There's no way to make everything "fit" in our life, even if we are trying to squeeze in fun, joyful things…things we want to do. There just isn't enough time and energy to go around. It's like a small child arriving at a theme park, overwhelmed with all the choices and sights and sounds and smells. Should we do the roller coaster first? Those funnel cakes smell so good–I want one! Maybe the roller coaster BEFORE the funnel cake is the smart move. Oh, but there's a show I want to see! And the parade is starting in an hour!

We can become overwhelmed with the options available to us, and those options are endless! Have you ever taken a day off of work "to relax" and then grown anxious trying to decide how to go about "relaxing"? You could watch TV! Or get a massage! Or a pedicure! Or take a nap! Or read a book! Or take a bubble bath! Or go for a hike! (Even typing out these choices is making me anxious!) You may even end up more frustrated at the end of the "day of relaxation" because you felt that no matter what you decided, it wouldn't be good enough. Whatever you choose, you're leaving out something else! The Fear of Missing Out (FOMO) is real…and it's strong.

The Sunk Cost Fallacy

Working with a coach, mentor, or therapist is a wonderful way to help understand what is worth holding onto, and what needs to be let go. A common misconception is that "letting go means I've given up." This is what's known as the "sunk cost fallacy": when we are hesitant to abandon or give up something because of what we have already invested (time, money, energy, etc.). Have you ever paid for something–like a meal or movie–and found yourself not enjoying it partway through, but then told yourself you've paid for it so you may as well finish it? This is an example of the sunk cost fallacy, which comes from our primitive brain (evidenced by lab data from rats who demonstrate similar behavior!). Another example is hesitating to leave a toxic work environment because we've spent so much time and energy there already. We invest so much of ourselves into relationships, jobs, roles, even meals that we later discover are not bringing us the joy we hoped for or are not aligned with our values. Letting these go may be necessary for us to break out of our own nautilus shell.

When we encounter these situations, it's helpful to remember that no matter what we choose moving forward, we CANNOT reclaim our prior investment of time, energy, or money. That investment is "sunk." We can't have it back, no matter how much we hold on. We can't control what's already been invested–"what's done is done." What we CAN control is how we respond and what next steps we take. We can reduce any future losses and take clear steps to invest our time, energy, and/or money more intentionally going forward. Often these situations are necessary for us to realize what's truly important, and they serve as data points for future decision-making.

Over the course of several sessions, one of my physician clients shared her frustration that some of her colleagues would make negative offhand remarks about her. Sometimes these comments were shared with her; other times, she would hear about them secondhand. While also advocating for her needs and creating and communicating boundaries with these colleagues, she told me that she "takes these very personally" and had difficulty with the emotions these comments created.

I asked her one of my favorite questions for my clients, "What do you need to let go of?" She told me that she needed to let go of these comments affecting her so deeply. She practiced this throughout the months that we worked together. During one session, she told me that she heard a negative comment that had been directed toward her, and she said, "I let it go. I went home so much lighter that day." By letting go of the negativity, she gained so much more: peace, lightness, and knowledge that her worth is not defined by what others think of her. Similarly, another physician client shared with me that, throughout her letting go process, she was more forgiving of herself and more peaceful.

One of my nurse practitioner clients shared with me that after a promotion, she became the supervisor of several other nurse practitioners with whom she previously had strong friendships. Her new role created some tension in the group, and she felt isolated from them and noticed they were treating her differently. She realized she couldn't control their behavior, but she could control her response. She chose to remove herself from their group chat to eliminate the tension created by the new dynamic. Afterwards, she shared with me that she "seemed to be thriving more." While it was difficult for her to let go of these personal relationships, doing so was necessary for her own well-being and for her growth as a team leader.

How does all of this relate to time management?

There are not enough hours in a day to do everything that is asked of us or demanded of us. We HAVE to let go of things, people, thoughts, or anything else that isn't serving us, or we can't spend our time intentionally. The more we can let go of what's not serving us, the more we invite in what IS serving us.

Action Step

Grab your journal and a pen and let's get into action. You can also reference the Purposeful MD downloadable journal (https://thepurposefulmd.com/book).

- Create a list of "what is no longer serving me." The list could be thoughts, objects (clothes are often a great example!), or people.
- What is one thing on this list that you can and will let go of?
- Write down any thoughts you have about letting go of this.
- Notice any resistance that comes up. Know that this is normal, natural, and part of the process.
- Commit to a plan for letting go. Write out detailed steps and put them on your calendar.
- Reach out for support along the way. Especially if it's a person you are letting go of, you will need some cheering on. I don't recommend ending a relationship with a person without support from a trusted loved one.
- After you have let go, notice the feelings in your body. Do you feel freer? Lighter? Less tense?
- Journal the feelings in your body and the thoughts that come up after you have let go.
- Be kind to yourself. This is not easy!

As a Flourishing Physician, you:

- Know that letting go of what's no longer serving you is a critical part of personal growth.
- Notice the resistance that comes up in the process of letting go.
- Recognize this resistance is our ego trying to keep us safe.
- Understand how the sunk cost fallacy can keep you stuck in situations that don't serve you.
- Commit to letting go when something isn't serving you.
- Take action on your insights!

Chapter 11
CELEBRATE YOURSELF

"Life was meant to be lived, and curiosity must be kept alive. One must never, for whatever reason, turn his back on life."
–Eleanor Roosevelt

As a medical director in my organization, one of my roles was leading our clinical quality and patient safety team. About 8 years ago, our team and senior leadership decided to pursue accreditation through The Joint Commission to validate our patient safety efforts. Anyone who has been through this type of preparation knows how time-consuming and challenging the process can be. After about a year and a half of intense and focused preparation, and a successful survey, we received notification that our organization was accredited. Of course, I was incredibly proud of this immense accomplishment.

About a year later, my physician colleagues and I gathered at a national conference, which was capped off with a beautiful formal dinner. At the dinner, my organization honored several physicians with awards called Values in Action, recognizing local leadership efforts. I was completely surprised to have been selected by my peers for the award for Performance, as a result of my work leading our Joint Commission preparation and accreditation. I accepted the award and gave a short (unplanned!) speech, then was welcomed and celebrated by my friends and colleagues immediately afterward. It didn't hurt that the conference was held in Las Vegas. After the ceremony, I put my luck to work at the poker tables (unsuccessfully, but it was fun to try).

Several weeks after the conference, my good friend and colleague invited me to meet her for dinner after work at a nearby restaurant. When I walked in, instead of meeting her at the table, the hosts directed me to the party room. Upon entering the room, I was floored to be met with a couple dozen of my colleagues and friends yelling, "Congratulations!" My team had planned a beautiful surprise reception to celebrate my award. I had no idea! I had never had any sort of surprise party or celebration thrown for me. I still remember how grateful and overcome with joy I felt in that moment. I wished I could bottle the feeling!

Over the years working with various coaches, they will often encourage me to celebrate when something goes well or when I accomplish something. Early on in my career, I found myself bristling at this suggestion. It felt too indulgent or selfish to celebrate myself. Since I trust my coaches, I eventually followed their guidance and began to celebrate even (and especially) the small wins. I noticed that taking the time to reflect on the wins or accomplishments allowed me to savor the good feelings and almost felt like bottling the joy!

I also realized that the celebration doesn't need to be grand. I don't have to throw myself a party every time I accomplish something. It can be as simple as saying to myself, "You did this thing that you didn't think you could do. This was a win!" Some wonderful ways to celebrate, that don't involve food, alcohol, or money, are:

- putting on upbeat music and having an impromptu dance party
- texting a friend to tell them about your accomplishment
- journaling about the accomplishment and how it makes you feel
- doing something just for you: taking a walk in nature, watching a show or movie by yourself, reading a book just for pleasure
- posting your accomplishment on social media and watching the "congrats" come pouring in
- dressing in clothing that makes you feel amazing
- choosing an image that reflects your accomplishment and adding it to your vision board
- engaging in a creative, playful activity for as long as you want

- making a "celebrate myself" playlist and/or a list of activities to do regularly to celebrate your awesome-ness (because really, you deserve to celebrate yourself DAILY)

It's so easy to get caught up in the day to day that we forget to stop and celebrate our accomplishments. Not only do we forget to celebrate our accomplishments–we don't often even think of our activities as accomplishments in the first place! One of my physician coaching clients recently shared that she felt like she was "operating at 60% capacity." I reminded her that, as a physician, mom, business owner, wife, and daughter, her 60% was someone else's 150%. She had been so used to how busy her life had become that it didn't occur to her just how much energy she was expending in all aspects of her life.

How often do we quickly move from one activity or task to the next, forgetting to stop and reflect? How often do we brush past our accomplishments, because we are going, going, going? Just like pushing past our strong emotions, our medical training rewarded us for moving through our day, from patient to patient or task to task, without stopping to think or process. We learned that the non-stop activity was necessary for us to function and succeed. It is not easy to break out of those ingrained patterns and try something new. Just as we discussed in the last chapter, if we can let go of these patterns, we open the door for new ways of thinking and being in the world.

One fun way to practice is to celebrate with my patients when they succeed at something. Patients love to be cheered on when they reach a goal. It can spur them to continue taking the steps to reach more goals. Some of my favorite memories during my clinical days were presenting a certificate or ribbon to a patient who had improved their blood sugar or blood pressure; it's so fun and joyful to share this achievement with them.

Similarly, I celebrate with my clients when they take an action that they didn't think they could do, or if they step into a fear and do something scary that gets them closer to what they want. Celebrating primes our reward center with a hit of dopamine, and we begin to intentionally adjust our behaviors to create more celebrations. Our brains are often primed toward the negative, but with continued practice, it becomes easier for us to focus on the positive and seek out those "feel-good emotions."

The Brag Board

I was coaching a nurse practitioner who was highly driven and accomplished but often struggled to acknowledge her own achievements. I see this frequently, especially in female clinicians; they place a high value on humility, to the extent that they "don't want to brag" about anything they have achieved. Unless we are aware of our own strengths and achievements, it's difficult for us to value ourselves and recognize our own self-worth.

During one session, I asked a client to create a "brag board" to bring to our next session two weeks later. The assignment was to write down everything about herself that she was proud of, everything she had accomplished, and everything she loved about herself. Part of the assignment was asking those closest to her to add to it as well: her husband, children, siblings, parents, close friends. She was skeptical and a bit nervous, as she was not used to seeking out compliments from others, but she agreed to the assignment.

At our next session, she showed me her "brag board" and how much fun she actually had creating it. I could immediately see how much happier she was during our video call. She said it was uncomfortable at first but incredibly empowering to clearly spell out all of her accomplishments. She loved the stories and feedback that others shared with her and she was grateful for having completed the exercise. She told me she planned to laminate the pages to save and to keep them somewhere close where she could read them when she was in a low mood. This exercise is one of my favorites to take clients through, as it is not something we do often enough!

Another client, a physician assistant leader, recognized the huge shifts in her mindset that she had been making over the course of our time together. After three months of coaching, she felt "more at peace" and "less guilty" about taking time for herself. She had been practicing managing her strong emotions and told me that her relationships with her husband and her adult son were stronger than ever. She was also spending less time charting and more time with her family. I encouraged her to celebrate herself, as the work she was doing was not easy. She came away with the insight that she needed to "give herself credit for progress."

One of my physician clients, who was fresh out of residency, shared her frustration that she wasn't getting enough feedback from her supervisors and physician leaders on her performance. She told me, "I need to feel like I'm getting an A." I pointed out that all the way through school and residency, she had been in an environment where she was visibly graded for her performance. Now, in a private practice environment, no one was "grading" her, and she was frustrated at the lack of feedback. I encouraged her to find ways to give the feedback to herself and celebrate her accomplishments, even in small ways and over small achievements.

How does all of this relate to time management?

Celebration gives us a great hit of dopamine that can keep us fueled during difficult moments. It allows us to tap into our common humanity and bolster our connection to others. When we celebrate ourselves, we validate our priorities and strengthen our ability to spend our time and energy on what's important to us.

Action Step

Grab your journal and a pen and let's get into action. You can also reference the Purposeful MD downloadable journal (https://thepurposefulmd.com/book).

(Credit for this practice goes to a mentor of mine, Dr. Pranay Parikh, who led this exercise in a mastermind I once attended.)

- What's a win that you had for today?
- What's a win that you had for this past week?
- What's a win that you had for this past year?
- These can be simple; just write whatever comes to mind. As you practice, it becomes easier to notice and to savor your wins throughout the day.
- Brainstorm ways you can celebrate your wins!
- Commit to an action to celebrate.
- Add it to your calendar.
- Notice how good that feels! Repeat regularly!

I'll give you a freebie: celebrate the fact that you are reading this book! Personal growth is not easy, which is why most people don't pursue it! You're bringing yourself up against some difficult emotions and some inner tension, which don't make for the smoothest journey. The fact that you are HERE–and you're doing this–is huge and worthy of celebrating!

As a Flourishing Physician, you:

- Recognize that the "small" wins are just as important in life as the "big" wins.
- Allow yourself to be celebrated and complimented by others.
- Celebrate yourself regularly and consistently.
- Celebrate others around you, knowing that celebration is infectious!
- Take action on your insights!

Chapter 12
YOU AS THE FLOURISHING PHYSICIAN

"The purpose of life is to live it, to taste experience to the utmost, to reach out eagerly and without fear for newer and richer experience."
–Eleanor Roosevelt

Amanda reached a breaking point where she didn't want to keep feeling the way she felt. She knew of a colleague who had started working with a professional coach, and that colleague told her how much the coaching reduced her stress. She asked her friend for a referral and reached out to the coach to set up an introductory call.

She felt immediately at ease with the coach. She felt she could tell the coach anything, and the coach wouldn't judge her but would honor where she was and help her reach that next step. The coach was a physician and had been through much of what she was now going through; she had "walked the walk." The coach had also come out on the other side–she had created the life that she wanted, the life that worked for her and her family. Amanda knew that working with this coach would be incredibly helpful and, hopefully, life-changing.

Her coach helped her to see where she could take some small initial steps, and create the confidence she needed to take even bigger steps to reach her goals. She challenged Amanda when she needed to, and she encouraged her and cheered her on when Amanda reached a milestone. Over the course of several months, Amanda's life began to change dramatically.

She realized she couldn't do it all. She needed help. She was not letting those in her life help her because she thought they couldn't do it as well as she could. She shared some of her thoughts with her husband, who had no idea how she felt. He was incredibly supportive because he just wanted her to be happy! She told her husband that she needed his help in very specific ways–to drop their daughter Chloe off at day care 3 days per week so she could exercise and to arrange for someone to clean their house every other week. She asked her parents to watch Chloe for two evenings each month so she and her husband could have a date night, just the two of them.

Next was her employer. Amanda wanted to ask for a scribe, but she knew that her employer would need to know how a scribe would benefit the practice. With her coach's help, Amanda researched and created a business case, demonstrating that she could increase her volume by two patients per day with the help of a scribe. This action would easily offset the cost of the scribe. It just so happened that the practice was able to transition one of their receptionists into a scribe, who began working with Amanda almost immediately.

Amanda's coach helped her to reduce the perfectionist thoughts that caused her to obsess over details of her charting. She began to allow herself to complete "good enough" charts. She asked for help from her staff with patient care-related tasks, and once her staff saw how much this would reduce her daily stress, they were happy to assist. Her staff also shared with her that they felt more fulfilled since they were able to have more ongoing contact with the patients.

Amanda began leaving work on time with her charts closed and patient messages addressed. She was able to focus on her family during evenings and weekends, and she found herself enjoying her time with her husband and daughter so much more. They even began to tackle a much-needed kitchen renovation, and the project brought her and her husband closer together and allowed her brain to focus on something outside of her job. When her best friend from college invited her to a girls' trip with 3 other friends a few months away, she said "yes" without hesitating.

Now Amanda is sleeping better and has more energy. Because her energy has increased, everything else in her life feels easier. She doesn't fall apart when her day gets thrown off, as she would have before. She's able to complete her tasks much more quickly. Her clinic staff and colleagues tell her she seems so much more calm and peaceful. She can feel it too–she never would have imagined feeling as grounded and joyful as she does now.

∼

If you're reading this book, you likely have many demands placed on your time and energy. These may include physician, mom, partner, daughter, friend, and possibly many more. Reading this book won't decrease the demands and pressure you're under. However, with the tools I've shared in this book, and the insights you've gained, you can navigate the demands with grace and with ease. We've discussed practicing empowering thoughts, managing strong emotions, setting and maintaining boundaries, learning to let go, and many other key concepts that can transform your mindset and your life.

My goals in writing this book are to share with you what I've learned and provide you with some tools that you can use in every aspect of your life. As you can see, my clients have used these tools with great success. Time management isn't just about being more efficient or using your time more effectively. There are so many aspects to time management that can help you flourish in your life. Working with a professional coach can be a wonderful and empowering way to take back control of your time, so that you control your schedule and your day, rather than the other way around. A good coach will support you and consistently remind you that you are always at choice, no matter what.

Remember, a Flourishing Physician:

- Knows her worth
- Lives life on her terms
- Lives a life she loves
- Prioritizes herself and her own needs
- Gets enough sleep and wakes up refreshed
- Manages her time and energy in a way that feels authentic
- Doesn't feel guilty spending time on things she enjoys
- Is fully present, no matter what she is doing
- Pursues hobbies and activities that light her up
- Lights her flame so she can light others' flames
- Believes in herself
- Has confidence in herself
- Values herself

A Flourishing Physician may be:

- a full-time practicing physician
- an attending at a teaching hospital
- a researcher
- an entrepreneur
- a real estate investor
- an author
- a speaker
- a coach
- any combination of the above

- much, much more

A Flourishing Physician looks different to everyone. What works for you may not work for your colleague or best friend from residency. What works for your coach or your practice partner may not work for you. When you take action toward your most purposeful life, and intentionally spend your time and energy on your values, your priorities, and your "why," you are creating joy at every turn.

I was recently coaching a physician who wanted advice on how to establish a morning routine. As a busy practicing physician, wife, and mother of two children under age 4, she had a slew of ideas she wanted to explore and pursue outside of medicine–entrepreneurship, real estate investing, writing, coaching, and many others–but she didn't know where to start. She told me, "I know I need some 'me' time and that has to be in the morning. It's the only time I can do it." She had convinced herself that the only way she could carve out time for herself was at 5 a.m. Her challenge was that her two small children frequently got into bed with her; while she enjoyed the snuggle time with them, she also recognized it disrupted her sleep. When 5 a.m. rolled around, she was too tired to get out of bed because her children had woken her up in the middle of the night.

As she talked, she was frequently using the word "should." I reflected this back to her, and she noted that she was judging herself for sleeping past 5 a.m. Throughout our conversation, she realized that she felt an immense pressure to "be a morning person" and use this as her "me time" when the reality was that with two small children, this may not be the best time for her to do so. She came up with a plan to carve out some time during her lunch hour and committed to set aside 30 minutes twice a week for quiet, creative, open time. She was much more excited about this plan. When we followed up, she had taken action and was on a path toward her goals.

If she had continued to force herself into this "morning person box," she never would have started down the path toward what she truly wanted. She would have only grown more frustrated because she wasn't doing what she thought she should have been doing. The same is true for you. Release yourself from the "shoulds" and the expectations and you will grow and flourish like you never expected.

That's one of the many reasons coaching is so powerful. A coach will ask you questions you've never thought of, to create a life that's better than you could have ever imagined. When you work with a coach, you unlock your own inner wisdom, your own inner knowing. You carve out the time and space just for YOU to create whatever you want, with the help of a professional. You give yourself permission to want things, and then you take action to get those things.

I love being a coach. I love empowering others–especially physicians and other medical professionals–to create the lives they love without guilt.

I celebrate you for reading this book and taking the action

steps described. You're already well on your way on this journey of reclaiming your time and reclaiming your life! You can find the journaling prompts at www.thepurposefulmd.com/book; you'll also find a discussion guide for reading the book in a book club.

I'm a firm believer in the power of coaching to change lives, and I want to give you a taste. To find out more, go to www.thepurposefulmd.com for helpful downloads and for information on how to connect with me.

Acknowledgements

This book is more than a simple project; it was a heartfelt journey made possible by the unwavering support from the amazing team at Writing Brave Press. To Brooke Adams Law, my incredible "book doula" who guided me through the birthing process of a book I never thought I could create; Meg Dippel, the overseer who always knew just the right words to nudge me forward; and Maria Webster, the marketing guru who sparked my imagination with innovative promotion ideas - thank you for saving me from countless hours of anguish and anxiety. Your help was truly a gift, and I am deeply grateful.

I am indebted to Dr. Errin Weisman for connecting me with Brooke, and to Dr. Shola Ezeokoli, Lisa Garber, and John Strasser for coaching me and encouraging me to embrace the identity of an author. A special thanks to Dr. Matt McGlothlin for his editing expertise and for reminding me to use more commas and fewer dashes.

I am eternally grateful to Dr. Peter Kim, Dr. Mike Woo-Ming, and the entire Momentum Mastermind for their incredible support, motivation, and guidance in setting goals and deadlines for this book. Your encouragement has been instrumental in ensuring this book reaches as many readers as possible.

My heartfelt gratitude goes out to my coaching clients for sharing their stories, vulnerability, and transformations with me. This book is a tribute to your courage and resilience, and I am honored to be a part of your journey.

To my friends and family who stood by me through the challenges of writer's block, your love and encouragement were my greatest inspiration. A special thank you to my mom for her steadfast admiration and belief in my writing, which fueled me to persevere even when I felt defeated.

To my children by choice, Jacqueline, Jalen, and Jenavi, your love and support have been my anchor. And to my daughter Emma and my husband Jacob, you are my rocks, my cheerleaders, and my greatest blessings. I am infinitely blessed and grateful to have you all in my life.

About the Author

Laura Suttin is a Board Certified family physician, a certified coach, a consultant, an author, a speaker, and an entrepreneur. She completed her medical training at the McGovern Medical School in Houston and her residency at the Christus Spohn Memorial Family Medicine Residency Program in Corpus Christi, Texas. She received her MBA from the University of Texas at Dallas in 2016.

Dr. Suttin began working with a coach many years ago, and found it so life-changing that she became a coach herself. She is certified through both the Physician Coaching Institute and The Insight Coaching Community. She launched Purposeful MD in 2021 with the mission of empowering physicians to create the lives they love without guilt. In her spare time she enjoys running, completing triathlons, traveling, and glamping with her family in their travel trailer. She lives in San Antonio with her husband and their four children.

Milton Keynes UK
Ingram Content Group UK Ltd.
UKHW021518200924
448513UK00014B/742

9 798987 370452